CHICAGO BEARS FACTS & TRIVIA

by

Wayne Mausser

The E. B. Houchin Company
1995

South Bend, Indiana

The E. B. Houchin Company
23700 Marquette Blvd. A-8
South Bend, Indiana 46628

Copyright 1995 by the Publisher on behalf of the Author

All rights reserved, which include the right
to reproduce this book or any portions thereof
in any form whatsoever without prior written consent
from the publisher.

ISBN: 0-938313-10-X

First Edition First Printing: September 1995

Cover Art by Peggy Eagan

Trading Cards from Author's Private Collection

Printed in USA

TABLE OF CONTENTS

THE BEAR FACTS	5
1. In the Beginning: 1920-24	7
2. The Second Crown: 1925-32	17
3. Halas Returns to the Helm: 1933-34	23
4. Up and Down: 1935-39	29
5. Sweet Revenge and Defeat: 1940-42	33
6. Hunk, Luke, and Paddy, But No Papa Bear: 1943-45	39
7. Climbing Back: 1946-50	43
8. Struggling: 1951-57	51
9. Papa Bear Returns Again: 1958-62	57
10. Champions: 1963	63
11. Tragedy and Inconsistency: 1964-67	67
12. The New Era: 1968-73	71
13. And Along Came Sweetness: 1974-81	79
14. The Iron Mike Era: 1982-92	87
15. Rebuilding Again: 1993-Present	93

A FEW GOOD BEARS	**97**
1. Mike Ditka	99
2. Dick Butkus	101
3. Gale Sayers	103
4. The Gallopin' Ghost	105
BEAR TRACKS	**107**
1. Chronology	109
2. The Bears vs. the NFL	119
BEAR ANSWERS	**121**
About the Author	**128**

The Bear Facts

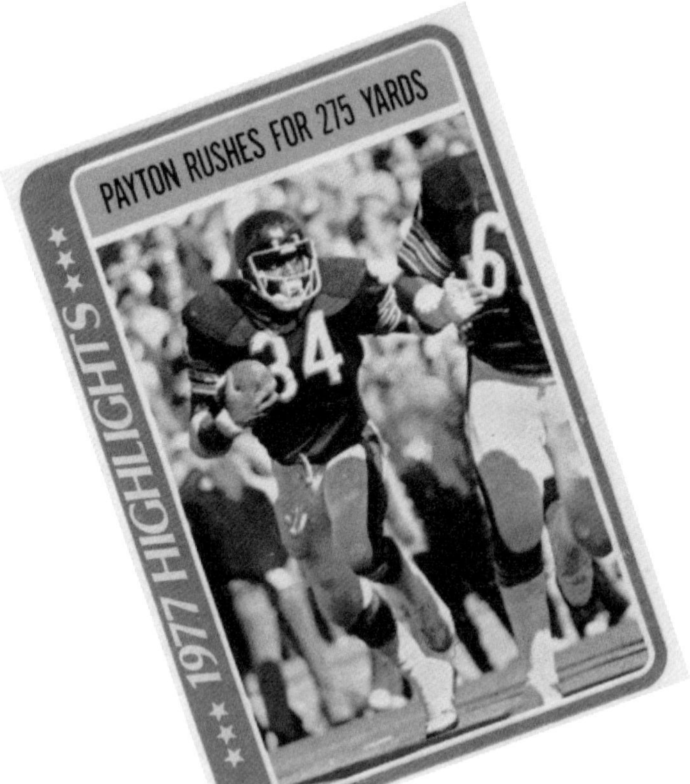
PAYTON RUSHES FOR 275 YARDS
1977 HIGHLIGHTS
34

1
In the Beginning: 1920-24

When you think of the Chicago Bears, one name immediately comes to mind: George Halas. But even before "Papa Bear", there were others involved who would set in motion the wheels that would bring Halas and the team that would later be known as the Bears together.

The principal player was A.E. Staley who owned a corn products plant called the A.E. Staley Company in Decatur, Illinois. Besides owning a profitable business, Staley encouraged his employees to get involved in athletics and sponsored different teams. Staley wanted good players who would also be good employees and felt he needed someone to recruit for him.

Over the Christmas holidays in 1919, Staley contacted Edward "Dutch" Sternaman, who was the top running back at the University of Illinois, and told him he needed someone like Dutch as a player and an organizer. However, Sternaman, who was a senior, was still pursuing his degree in mechanical engineering and wanted to continue school. He told Staley he was interested though and said he would give it some thought.

Staley was not a man to wait around. He had heard of George Halas, that Halas was not only good at football but had also been a professional baseball player. By this time, Halas had already graduated from the University of Illinois where he had played several sports and had served in the U.S. Navy as a member of the Great Lakes Naval Training Station football team during the last year of World War I. After the war, he had a brief Major League Baseball career, then went to work for the Chicago, Burlington & Quincy Railroad, and in the fall of 1919, he also had played with the Hammond Pros, a professional team that was owned and operated by Dr. A.A. Young as a hobby.

In March 1920, Halas was contacted by a representative of the A.E. Staley Company. The president of the firm wanted him to consider an offer to work for Staley as well as to play for its baseball and football teams along with coaching the football team. The 25-year-old Halas jumped at the idea, and when he met A.E. Staley, details of their agreement were worked out. Besides being involved in athletics, Halas would also learn how to make corn starch, the company's chief product.

That summer Halas played baseball, made corn starch, and started recruiting for football and devising plays. Also taking a job with the Staleys at the end of that June was Dutch Sternaman, who joined Halas in recruiting young men to work for the Staley Company and to play football. The two agreed to share coaching duties. Some of the names on that 1920 Staley team were Guy Chamberlain, Ralph Scott, Jimmy Conzelman, Hugh Blacklock, Burt Ingwerson, Ross Petty, Randy Young, Roy Adkins, Pard Pierce, and Bob Koehler. There were only a couple of holdovers from the previous year: Charlie Dressen, who would later go on to baseball fame, Walter Veach, and Jack Mintun.

Before the season was to begin, a very important meeting took place. Halas and representatives of nine other football teams met at Ralph Hay's Hupmobile showroom in Canton, Ohio, on September 17, 1920. Halas represented the Decatur Staleys and from that meeting, the American Professional Football Association was born.

The league set a membership fee of one hundred dollars. Besides the Staleys, 13 other teams were given franchises, but one later withdrew. The league was looking for a big name to serve as president, and Jim Thorpe was elected.

A few weeks later the season began and the Staleys shut out the Moline Indians, 3-0, and went on to finish a very successful 10-1-2. Their only loss was to the Chicago Cardinals, 7-6. One interesting note from that first season is that the teams would only travel to nearby cities to play because of the cost of transportation. No official standings were kept that first year, but if a league champion was crowned, it would have been the Akron Pros, who were undefeated. Dutch Sternaman led the Staleys in scoring, and the season should be termed a success. Here are the results.

Chicago Bears Facts & Trivia 9

O	3	Moline	20	0	W
O	10	Kewaunee	25	7	W
O	17	@ Rock Island Indep.	7	0	W
O	24	@ Chicago Tigers	10	0	W
O	31	@ Rockford	29	0	W
N	7	@ Rock Island Indep.	0	0	T
N	11	@ Champaign	20	0	W
N	14	@ Minneapolis Marines	3	0	W
N	21	Hammond Pros	28	7	W
N	25	@ Chicago Tigers	6	0	W
N	28	@ Chicago Cardinals	6	7	L
D	5	@ Chicago Cardinals	10	0	W
D	12	Akron Indians	0	0	T

Financially, each player on the Staleys made an average of about $125 per game. They were also paid their salary of $50 weekly while working as a Staley employee. Supposedly, Guy Chamberlain was the highest paid player, making $1,650, while Dutch Sternaman and George Trafton were each paid $1,618. Halas was paid extra because of his dual role as player/coach and made $2,322.77.

That first season with the Staleys only solidified Halas's feelings about football and what he wanted to do with his future. He no longer had aspirations about any other occupation except staying involved with football.

But 1921 was quite different than the previous year. A.E. Staley loved athletics and competition; that was why he started sports programs for his employees. But he was also a good businessman and shrewd enough to know that continuing football in Decatur was not going to be a profitable venture. So, Staley called Halas into his office in the early fall of 1922 and made young George an offer he couldn't refuse. Staley suggested that Halas take the team to Chicago where it would be more financially feasible to operate. He also gave George $5,000 in seed money to operate the team for the season. Halas jumped at the opportunity and an agreement was drawn up on October 6, 1921.

So the Decatur Staleys moved to Chicago. Halas had made arrangements will William Veeck, Sr., the president of the Chicago Cubs Baseball Club, to use Cubs Park, now known as Wrigley Field. That led to a relationship that would last until the end of 1970. In the first season at Wrigley Field (then known as Cubs Park), the team would continue to be known as the Staleys. That was part of the agreement, which is as follows.

> A.E. Staley Manufacturing Company-Corn Producers
> Decatur, Illinois
> October 6, 1921
>
> The Staley Football Team
> Decatur, Illinois
>
> Gentlemen:
> Confirming our verbal agreement with you, we agree to place the names of all your football players (Total number not to exceed nineteen) on our payrolls at a salary of $25.00 per week with the exception of those already being taken care of in that manner on regular jobs.
> We also agree to enter into an advertising contract with you whereby we undertake to pay you Three Thousand ($3,000) Dollars for such advertising in your score book as you have suggested.
> It is our wish and plan that when the football team goes to Chicago on October 15th, it remain there until the end of the season.
> In this event while the team is in Chicago we will maintain on the payroll the entire nineteen men on the team at $25.00 per week until this company shall have paid you in total, including both advertising and salary amounts, the sum of Five Thousand ($5,000.00) Dollars.
> In consideration of these various payments, it is agreed that the team is to operate under the name of "The Staley Football Club". That you are to use your best efforts to disseminate information regarding, and to facilitate the business of the A.E. Staley Manufacturing Company; that you are to secure the utmost publicity in the newspapers for the team and the company; that you are to so conduct the team, its playing and management as to reflect credit upon the A.E. Staley Manufacturing Company; that you will enter into no contracts or obligations in any way binding upon the A.E. Staley

Manufacturing Company with this present exception.
It is understood that this arrangement shall terminate at the end of the present football season.
Please indicate your acception of the provisions of this agreement. I remain.

The agreement was signed by both A.E. Staley and George Halas. The final game in Decatur was against Rock Island on October 10, which was the first game of the regular season and only four days after George Halas signed the contract to take over the team. The Staleys held on for a 14-10 win and then it was off to Chicago. On October 16, the Staleys won at Wrigley Field, 16-13, over the Rochester Jeffersons. The 1921 Staleys were the American Professional Football Association champs, with a 9-1-1 record. Their only loss was to the Buffalo All Americans, 7-6. The tie came once again in the last game of the season, this time against the Cardinals.

George Halas took on a partner that season. Dutch Sternaman and Halas now each shared 50 percent of the team. The 1921 team was not very successful financially, but it ended up losing only $71.63.

The agreement with Staley ended after the 1921 season, so Halas and Sternaman knew they had their work cut out for them. One of the first things they did was change the name of the franchise to the Chicago Bears. That was done on January 28, 1922. On May 2, Halas and Sternaman filed for incorporation for a $20 fee and a franchise tax of $13.34. Halas and Sternaman were listed on the teams board of directors along with one other person who was associated with another team! Paddy Driscoll, who played on the crosstown rival Cardinals, was named to the Bears board of directors. Actually, Halas and Sternaman hoped this little honor would convince Paddy to play with them. Driscoll was one of the best players in league, and he always gave the Halas and Sternaman fits on the field. But league president Joe Carr stepped in and told them that they could not tamper with Driscoll unless the Cardinals approved. That didn't happen, so in September of that year, Driscoll's name was removed from the Bears board of directors. As for titles within the organization, it was agreed that Halas and Sternaman would serve as president and secretary, respectively, then each year switch the roles.

In assembling the 1922 team, one key player was lost. Guy Chamberlain left for the Canton Bulldogs to assume a dual role as player and coach. Also leaving for Canton was John "Tarzan" Taylor. One player who did not leave on his own was Chick Harley and that resulted in the Bears' first lawsuit. According to the Chicago *Tribune*, "The suit contends that Chick Harley was the unremitting object of attempts to belittle his playing ability, that the Staleys' line gave way in games of 1921 in order to let opposing players spill him, and that he was driven into a state of mental collapse by the 'freeze out' treatment which culminated in the team's refusal to accept his insertion into the second half of the game with Buffalo late in the 1921 season, with 10,000 people looking on. For months following this episode, Chick Harley was in a sanitarium."

However, the case did not go to court. Reportedly, the judge in the case asked Sternaman what the Bears' net worth was, and he replied with a shrug, "Eleven jocks in the locker room." Apparently, there were no O.J. Simpson attorneys present because nothing became of the case. For some reason, Harley and his brother had not signed a formal contract with Halas and Sternaman, the previous year.

One player the Bears did add in 1922 was Joey Sternaman, Dutch's younger brother. Joey was only 5'6", but he was fast, tough and durable, and he became the Bears' starting quarterback. He was also one of the best drop-kickers in the league over the next nine years.

The Bears also made their first player deal midway through the season, buying the contract of tackle Ed Healey from the Rock Island Independents for $100.

The Bears opened up the 1922 season at Cubs Park against the Racine Legion and won, 6-0. They finished 9-3, losing to the Canton Bulldogs, 7-0, the Chicago Cardinals, 6-0, and again to the Cardinals in the final game of the season, 9-0. The Bears outscored their opponents 123-44, but ended in second place behind the Canton Bulldogs.

The Sternamans scored the majority of the teams points, with Dutch scoring 41 and Joey accounting for 32. The Bears made a modest profit of $1,476.92.

In 1923, the Bears lost Joey Sternaman to the Duluth Kelleys, but they did sign Oscar Knop along with Frank Hanny and Johnny Bryan. Chicago lost two of its first five games but finished strong at 9-2-1. However, Canton went undefeated and won the league title for the second straight year.

In 1924, the Canton Bulldogs were sold to the owner of the

Cleveland team, who only wanted most of the Canton players, not the Canton franchise; by purchasing the team, he also became owner of the players' contracts. The Bears were able to make a little money after expenses. Chicago added Jim McMillen, a guard from the University of Illinois, and went into the season with hopes of winning the title. But the Bears started slowly, losing their first game to the Packers, followed by two straight ties. Chicago finished 6-1-4 but once again finished second behind the Bulldogs, this time out of Cleveland. The Bears did play three games after the regular season ended, but they did not count officially.

Even though Chicago did not win the championship, it did show a profit of $20,000.

What about those early years?

1. When was George Halas born?

2. What were his parents' names?

3. What university did Halas attend?

4. Halas played briefly as a Major League Baseball player. Name the team he played for, the position he played, and the player who succeeded him at that position.

5. What position did Guy Chamberlain play?

6. What was Heartley Anderson's nickname?

7. How many points did the Staleys score in 1920?

8. How many points did the Staleys' opponents score in 1920?

9. Ralph Scott was an All-American at what position?

10. Randy Young and Roy Adkins attended what college?

11. What position did Adkins play?

12. What position did Young play?

13. In 1921, what Chicago hotel did Halas, Sternaman, and most of the Bears players live in?

14. George Halas is credited with inventing what offensive formation?

15. In 1923, Halas returned a fumble 98 yards for a touchdown. Who fumbled the ball?

16. What position did Halas play in the 1919 Rose Bowl Game between his team, Great Lakes Naval Training Center, and the Marines?

17. How long did Halas play for the Staleys and the Bears?

18. Halas's first championship came in 1921. When was his second?

19. How many championships did Halas win as a coach?

20. How many wins did Halas have?

21. What number did Halas wear?

22. In what year did Halas step down as coach for the last time?

23. Chick Harley had a brother who was his manager. Who was he?

24. What did it cost the Staleys to rent Cubs Park?

25. Who won the first Chicago Staleys-Green Bay Packers game?

26. What was the score?

27. Where was the game played?

28. Who scored the Staleys' touchdowns?

29. What position did Ken Huffine play?

30. How many years did he play with Chicago?

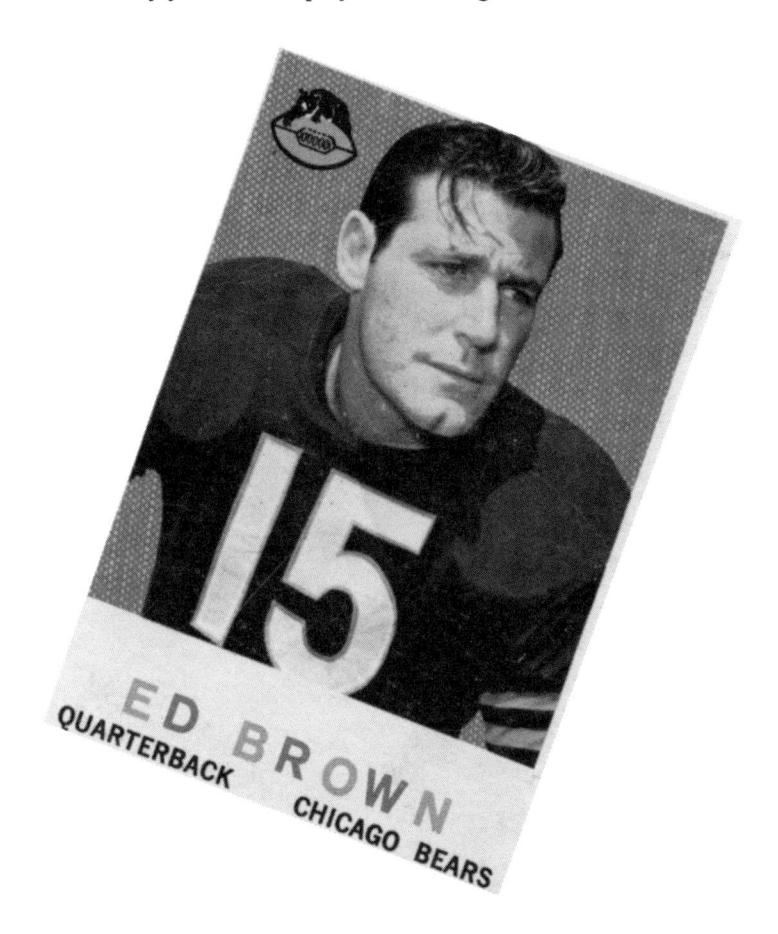

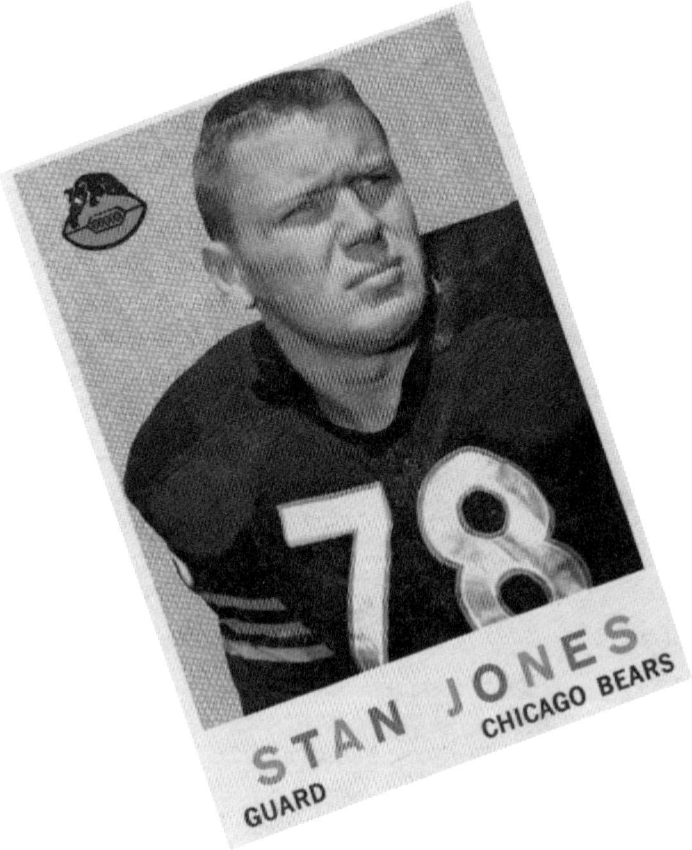
78
STAN JONES
GUARD
CHICAGO BEARS

2
The Second Crown: 1925-32

The 1926 Bears went 12-1-3 but did not win the title. After that season, the league declined from 22 teams down to 12. Some of the teams that dropped out were the Milwaukee Badgers, Canton Bulldogs, Detroit Panthers, Akron Indians, Columbus Tigers, and Hammond Pros.

Besides losing teams, the NFL was being raided for players by the new American Football League. The Bears lost Grange and Joey Sternaman, so they went out and signed the league's top all purpose back, Paddy Driscoll, from the Cardinals. Chicago bought Driscoll's contract for $3,500, then signed him to a contract that would guarantee him $10,000 a year. Other new players were acquired, and to get them in the lineup, both Halas and Sternaman took themselves out of the starting unit.

As the season went along, it became apparent the Bears could win without Grange and Sternaman. Chicago was undefeated when they faced the Frankford Yellow Jackets at Shibe Park in Philadelphia. The Yellow Jackets were 12-1-1 going in, while the Bears were 11-0-2. Chicago led 6-0 with less than two minutes left when tailback Hust Stockton threw a 27-yard touchdown pass to the smallest man on the field, 5' 5", 144 pound "Two Bits" Homan. Tex Hamer made good on the extra point, and the victory went to the Yellow Jackets. The Bears won their next game and tied the last game but the title was decided in the loss to Frankford.

In 1927, the Bears finished 9-3-2 after winning their first five games. Joey Sternaman was back with the Bears that year and regained his starting quarterback job. One of those early victories was a 12-0 win over the New York Yankees at Wrigley Field on October 16. The win was the Bears third straight, but even more significantly, the Game's biggest player, Red Grange, suffered a severe knee injury. Even though Grange returned after missing four games, the injury caused him to miss the next season, and he would never be the same open-field runner again. As for Chicago, two straight losses to the Cardinals and Giants meant a third place finish.

The following season saw the league reduced from 12 to 10 teams. The Cleveland Bulldogs and Duluth Eskimos dropped out that year. The Bears started out with a 15-0 win over the Cardinals in what would be the last game for the legendary Jim Thorpe. However, Chicago would suffer a two-game losing streak twice during the season and would finish up 7-5-1, which landed them in fifth place in the 10-team league.

In 1929, the Bears sank even further, finishing a dismal 4-9-2, after starting the year by going 4-1-1. Red Grange returned as a defensive back and played well, but George Halas retired. The Green Bay Packers won the title, going 12-0-1. One of the biggest embarrassments for Chicago was a 40-6 loss to the Cardinals. Ernie Nevers scored all of his team's points in that romp, including rushing for six touchdowns. The Bears record dropped them into ninth place in what was now a 12-team league. It was the worst season ever for George Halas and Dutch Sternaman, and some changes were needed.

The collapse of the '29 Bears was symbolic to what was happening to the economy as "The Great Depression" began. The 1930 season marked the first of several sojourns from coaching by George Halas. During the previous year, Halas and Sternaman had a lot of disagreements, and after the season, both men agreed that the Bears should be coached by one man and not either of them. So they hired Ralph Jones, who had been head coach at Lake Forest College, near Chicago. He also had coached both men at the University of Illinois. Jones can be credited with developing the Split-T formation in 1930. Personnel wise, 35-year-old Paddy Driscoll did not return, but some of the other Bears did come back. Veterans George Trafton, Joey Sternaman, Link Lyman, and Laurie Walquist returned for Jones, but they were all in their 30s by now. One of the newcomers, though, turned out be Bronko Nagurski, a future Hall-of-Famer. Nagurski's $5,000 salary was the highest on the team.

The Bears and their new coach got off to a slow start, playing the

Brooklyn Dodgers to a scoreless tie. The next week Chicago was shut out by the Packers. The Bears finally won in the third game of the season, 20-0, over the Minneapolis Red Jackets before being shut out by the Giants the following week, 12-0. But after that 2-3-1 start, Chicago won seven of its next eight games to finish at 9-4-1. The Bears outscored their opponents, 165-72, and posted five shutouts, including a 21-0 whitewash of the eventual league champion Packers.

In 1931, Chicago slipped to 8-5, finishing third behind the Portsmouth (Ohio) Spartans and Curly Lambeau's Green Bay Packers, who won their third straight title. Some highlights in the season were a last second victory over the Giants and a 7-6 win over Green Bay in the next to last game of the season.

Finally, in 1932, the Bears won their second title. Chicago finished 6-1-6 during the regular season, and since tie games did not figure into the winning percentage, the Bears advanced on to the title game against Portsmouth. Portsmouth was 6-1-4 and had the same winning percentage as the Bears. Green Bay finished 10-3-1, good enough for third place.

In the first playoff game to decide a league championship, Chicago and Portsmouth met indoors at the Chicago Stadium. The field was not the normal 100 yards long, but instead only 80. Because the spectators were only a few feet away from the sideline, any ball that was downed within 10 yards of a sideline or a ball that went out of bounds was brought 10 yards inbounds for the following play. Most football historians agree that this game marked the beginning of hash marks in professional football. Actually, the indoor arena had a pretty good playing surface for the game. Just a week before, a circus had performed there, and there was still about six inches of dirt on the cement. Sod was then laid on top.

A crowd of more than 11,000 turned out to watch the game, and Portsmouth had a disadvantage going in. Dutch Clark, who was the team's tailback and kicker and who also led the league in scoring, was unable to play. But it wasn't because of an injury. You see, Clark was also the basketball coach at Colorado College and had to be at the school to begin his coaching duties. Fullback Ace Gutowsky was moved to fill Clark's spot.

The first three quarters of the game were scoreless, but then the Bears broke through in the fourth. Defensive back Dick Nesbit intercepted a Gutowsky pass on the Spartan side of the field and ran it down to the seven yard line. On a fourth and two, Bronko Nagurski lobbed a touchdown pass to Red Grange. The Bears converted the extra point and later recorded a safety to come away with a 9-0 win. Chicago would be a dominant team in the NFL for the next 15 years. But for coach Ralph Jones, it would be his last game as Bears coach.

What about those years?

1. Bears center George Trafton took up another sport in the late 1920s. What was it?

2. What Bear led the league in receiving in 1932?

3. How many passes did this league-leader catch in 1932?

4. What college did Bronko Nagurski attend?

5. Who recruited Nagurski for college?

6. How many rushing touchdowns did Nagurski have in 1930?

7. This player was signed by Chicago in late 1930 which prompted the team to be fined. Who was this player?

8. What college did this signee attend?

9. What position did this signee play?

10. How many regular season games did this signee play for the Bears in 1930?

11. How many years did this signee play for Chicago?

12. What position did Keith Molesworth play?

13. What college did Molesworth attend?

14. How many years did Molesworth play with the Bears?

15. Who led Chicago in scoring in 1930?

16. How many points did the high scorer have in 1930?

17. How many touchdowns did the 1930 high scorer score?

18. Who caught the winning touchdown pass for the Bears in a 12-6 win over the Giants in 1931?

19. How long did this player play for Chicago?

20. What position did he play?

21. What team gave Chicago its only loss in 1932?

22. What was the score of that single?

23. How many scoreless ties did the Bears have in 1932?

24. How many points did the Bears score in their first four games?

25. Don Murry played on the 1932 championship team. What position did he play?

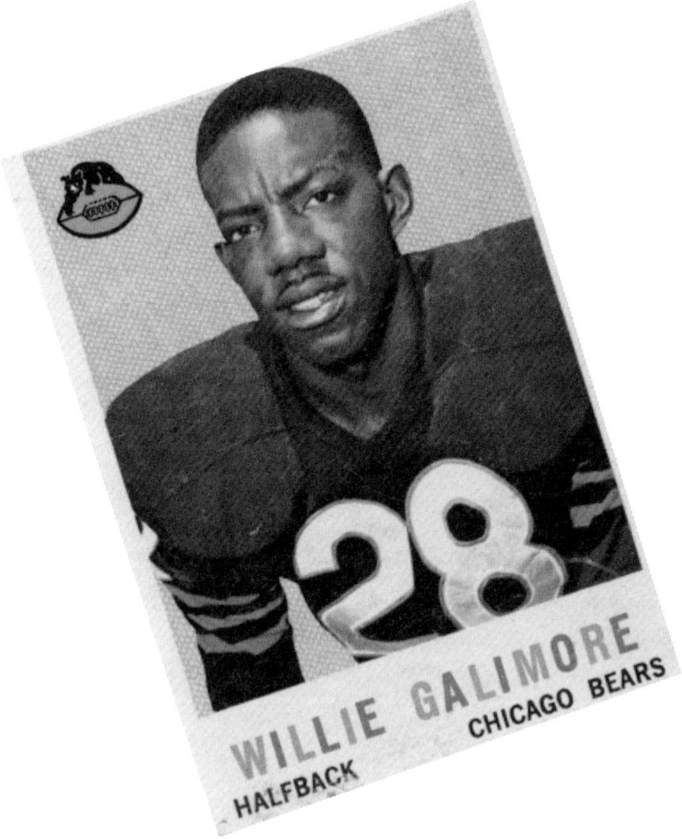
WILLIE GALIMORE
HALFBACK
CHICAGO BEARS

3
Halas Returns to the Helm: 1933-34

When coach Ralph Jones resigned after the 1932 season, George Halas came back as coach. This marked the first time that Halas would be the sole coach of the Bears. When he took over the reins again, Halas said it would just be for one year, but that, of course, would not be the case.

Three rule changes were introduced during the February 1933 NFL owners meeting, and all were adopted. The first change would alter the course of pro football. The owners decided to allow the quarterback to throw a forward pass from anywhere behind the line of scrimmage. Thus, the passing game was really born. Another rule change moved the goal posts up to the goal lines, which would encourage more field goal attempts. The third change declared that the hashmarks would be chalked 10 yards in from the sidelines. Those hashmarks would be used any time a ball was downed within five yards of a sideline or if it went out of bounds. The owners were excited about the changes because scoring was expected to increase which would liven up the game for the fans and increase their interest.

Halas went out and added some new players to hopefully pump some more offense in the Bears game. He signed placekicker Jack Manders and offensive lineman George Musso, and he designed a fake plunge and jump pass for Bronko Nagurski.

The Bears were not expected to do well in 1933, but they began the season by winning their first six games. But then the Bears' offense came to a halt, as they lost their next game on the road, 10-0, to the

Redskins, tied the Eagles, 3-3, then were shutout by the Giants, 3-0. However, the Bears rebounded and won their next four games, three of which were at home, to finish at 10-2-1, good for first in the NFL West. Chicago would play the New York Giants in the first divisional NFL Championship game, and it would be played on a cold, damp, muddy surface at Wrigley Field, in front of only 26,000 fans.

The game went back and forth before the Bears scored late in the fourth quarter on a lateral from Bill Hewitt to Bill Karr. The Giants nearly scored on the last play of the game, but wingback Dale Burnett was stopped by the cagey veteran, Red Grange, who anticipated a Burnett lateral to teammate Mel Hein. Grange hit Burnett high, pinning his arms and preventing the lateral.

The Bears had now won two straight titles. Could they make it three in a row? As it turned out, the 1934 team was one of the greatest in Chicago's history and perhaps one of the best teams of that era. A key addition to the Bears attack, was halfback Beattie Feathers, who at 5'10" and 185 pounds, had both speed and power. With that combination, he became the first rusher to gain over one thousand yards in a season, finishing with 1,004.

Some more innovations in 1934. First the league introduced a more streamlined football, replacing what George Halas called the "Cantaloupe shaped ball." The new aerodynamic shape was more conducive to the passing game. It also put an end to the drop kick, which had been a big part of the Bears offense. One other change allowed place kickers to use the dirt as a sort of kicking tee, which Halas reasoned should help his own kicker, Jack Manders.

Also in 1934 the first College All-Star Game was played. Nearly 80,000 fans at Soldier Field in Chicago witnessed a scoreless tie between the Bears and the College All-Stars.

But Chicago's offense would come alive during the regular season and through the first nine games, just one team would come within 13 points. The Bears finished a perfect 13-0, with the last two games, hard fought 19-16 and 10-7 wins over the Detroit Lions. Once again the Bears were undisputed champions of the NFL West, and they traveled to Manhattan to take on the 8-5 New York Giants, champions of the NFL East. The Bears had beaten the Giants twice during the regular season and were heavy favorites to win their third straight title. But it was not meant to be. Chicago had lost Beattie Feathers late in the season when he suffered a shoulder separation against the Cardinals.

On the day of the game, it was only nine degrees above zero and the field at the Polo Grounds was covered with a thin coating of ice. The Bears took a 10-3 lead at halftime on a touchdown by Bronko Nagurski and the extra point and field goal by Jack Manders. But the Giants were a little more sure footed than Chicago in the second half. With the help of gym shoes, the New Yorkers were able to run by the sliding Chicago defenders and in the last 10 minutes of the game, New York scored four touchdowns to win, 30-13. While the Giants celebrated, the Bears were stunned at the sudden turn of events. The "Sneakers Championship" was a sad finale to the best season in Bears history, up to that point. After the season, Red Grange and Link Lyman retired, marking the end of the Bears' first real dynasty.

What about those years?

1. What school did placekicker Jack Manders come from?

2. What was Manders's nickname?

3. Manders led the league in scoring in 1934. How many points did he have?

4. Manders led the league in extra points in 1933. How many did he have?

5. Beginning with the opening game of the 1933 season and continuing through part of the 1937 season, how many consecutive extra points did Manders kick?

6. In 1934, Manders established a record for field goals in a season. How many did he kick?

7. Who broke Manders's field goal record, how many field goals did he kick, and in what year did he break the record?

8. Where did halfback Beattie Feathers attend college?

9. Feathers's average yards per carry in a season was a league record. What was it?

10. What was Feathers's lifetime yards per carry average with Chicago?

11. How many seasons did Feathers spend with the Bears?

12. Where does Feathers currently rank on the all-time Bears rushing list?

13. How many career touchdowns did Feathers score?

14. What was the Bears' College All-Star Game record?

15. The College All-Star Game was whose brainchild?

16. How many College All-Star Games did the Bears play in?

17. In what year did the Bears lose to the College All-Stars?

18. What was the score of the game that the Bears lost to the College All-Stars?

19. Guard Joe Kopcha played five seasons with the Bears. How many times was he named an All-Pro?

20. "Bull" Doehring had what unusual talent?

21. What was Doehring's first name?

22. How many years did Doehring play with the Bears?

23. End Bill Hewitt never wore what protective gear?

24. In the 1933 championship game between the Bears and the Giants, Chicago scored the winning touchdown when Hewitt lateraled the ball to Bill Karr, who scored the winning touchdown. Who passed the ball to Hewitt?

Chicago Bears Facts & Trivia

25. What Bear made the block that took out two Giant defenders on that winning play?

26. How much money did each Bear receive for winning the 1933 championship?

27. How many shutouts did the Bears have in 1933 and who were they against?

28. Who was the Giants' coach in the memorable "Sneakers" championship game of 1934?

29. Where did the sneakers come from?

30. What team came closest to beating the Bears in their undefeated season of 1934?

31. What was the score of the Bears' closest game in 1934?

32. Who quarterbacked the Bears in 1934?

33. What college did the Bears' 1934 quarterback attend?

34. When was the 1934 quarterback's first Bear season?

35. How many years did this quarterback play with Chicago?

36. What WGN radio announcer did the play-by-play of the 1933 championship game?

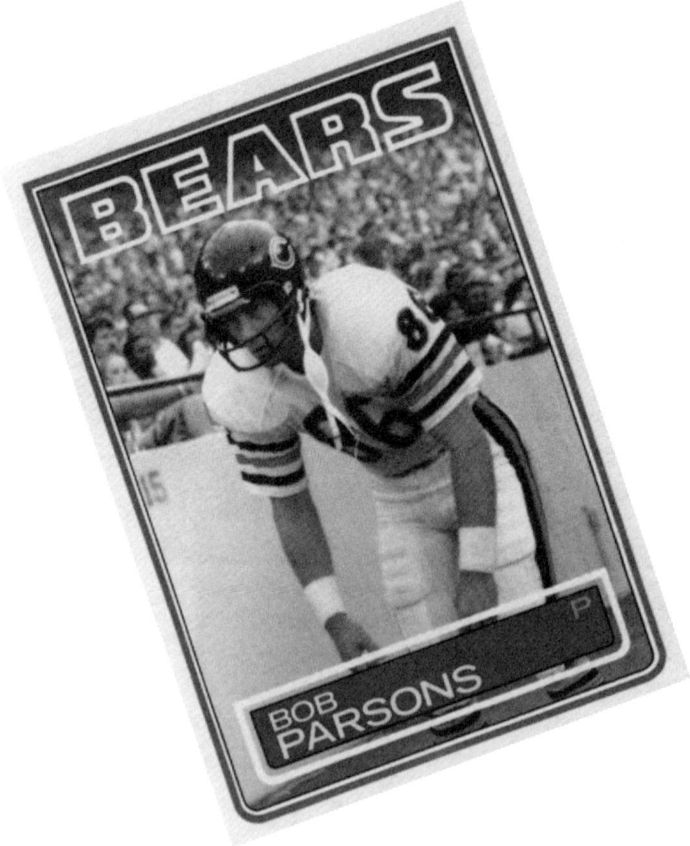
BEARS
P
BOB
PARSONS

4
Up and Down: 1935-39

After a nearly perfect but disappointing 1934 season, the Bears had no reason to believe they would slip the following year. But that was not to be the case. Bronko Nagurski missed most of the season because of a growth on his hipbone, and Beattie Feathers was still hampered by a shoulder injury suffered late in the previous season. Plus, starting quarterback Carl Brumbaugh decided to retire, and he was replaced by backup Bernie Masterson.

Everything was tough for the Bears in 1935. It started with a hard fought 5-0 win over the College All-Stars, and it continued through the regular season, as Chicago slipped to 6-4-2.

Actually, the Bears played pretty well in the first half of the season. After an opening game loss to the Packers, Chicago reeled off three straight wins before losing to Green Bay again. Then after two straight wins, the Bears were shutout by the Giants, 3-0. Then came a tie, a loss, another tie, and finally a shutout win over the Cardinals.

Chicago wound up third in the NFL West, while the Packers came in second. Detroit finished 10-2 to win its first NFL title.

After the 1935 season, it was decided there would be a draft of graduating college seniors. The annual draft began in 1936 with the Eagles having the first choice. The Bears ended up with a good draft, with two of their selections eventually making it into the Pro Football Hall of Fame.

In 1936, there was a new American Football League, but it only survived two seasons. The NFL was stable that year and had no franchises move. Also, for the first time, all of the teams in the league would play the same number of games.

The Bears won their first six games and finished 9-3. In the seventh game, the Packers beat Chicago at Wrigley Field and went on to win the title game over the Redskins.

The next year, 1937, the Bears improved to 9-1-1. They won their first six games before being tied, 3-3, by the Giants. The next week, the Packers won at Wrigley Field, 24-14, behind the passing combination of Arnie Herber and end Don Hutson. But the Bears bounced back to win their last four games to win the western division. In the championship game, the Redskins behind Sammy Baugh beat the Bears 28-21 in Chicago. "Slingin' Sammy" was 18 of 33, for 335 yards and three TDs.

In 1938, the Bears dipped to 6-5. The rushing and kicking games were weak; Manders had only three field goals, and Chicago's record was its worst since 1929.

In 1939, the Bears rebounded to an 8-3 record and finished one game behind the Packers. Coach Halas and Clark Shaughnessy worked on modernizing the split-T-formation, believing it would be the most effective tool for using the pass.

Of course, Halas needed a quarterback, so he arranged a trade with Art Rooney, the owner of the Pittsburgh Pirates, who would later become the Steelers. Rooney made quarterback Sid Luckman his first draft choice, then traded him to the Bears. Luckman would go on to become one of the great quarterbacks in the league, and the Bears would be starting one of the most exciting eras in their history.

What about those years?

1. Who was the player from the University of Alabama, who played against the Bears in the 1935 College All-Star Game, then played professionally with the Green Bay Packers?

2. Who was the center from Michigan in that same College All-Star game?

3. This quarterback from North Dakota would later come to be known as "Mr. Chicago". Who was he?

4. Who were the three Bears that were named All-Pro for the 1935 season?

5. What positions did these three All-Pros play?

6. Who was the Bears' first pick in the 1936 draft?

7. What college did their first draft pick come from?

8. The Bears' last pick in the 1936 draft was one of two players taken that year who would make it to the Pro Football Hall of Fame. Who was he?

9. What position did this last pick, Hall-of-Famer play?

10. What college did this last pick, Hall-of-Famer attend?

11. What was the nickname of Bears' end Edgar Manske?

12. What team was Manske acquired from?

13. Who was the Bears' first round draft pick in 1937?

14. What position did the Bears' Number 1 1937 pick play?

15. What college was the Bears' Number 1 1937 pick from?

16. In 1931, Halas traded Bill Hewitt for a first round draft selection. Name the team that Hewitt was traded to.

17. Who did the Bears receive for Hewitt?

18. What position did this acquisition play?

19. In 1937, the Bears and the Cardinals set a record for most points scored in a regular season game. The game was won by the Bears. What was the final score?

20. What was an oddity about this high scoring game?

21. Placekicker Jack Manders scored the Bears' first points against the Redskins in the championship game of 1937. How did he score?

22. Manders also had the Bears' second score. How did he do it?

23. Besides being a professional football player, what other professional sport did Bronko Nagurski play?

24. Bears' guard Joe Stydahar had the distinction of being a star in this annual game that began in 1939. What was this game?

25. The Bears' leading rusher in 1939 was a first round pick from Holy Cross. Who was he?

26. How many yards did this first rounder gain in 1939?

5

Sweet Revenge and Defeat: 1940-42

By 1940, the sentiment toward professional football had changed. In the 1920s, it had been looked upon as a game that corrupted college players. But by the end of the 1930s, it was thought of as respectable and now exciting because of the development of the forward pass. The world may have been on the brink of war, but the fans were filling the stadiums on Sunday.

The Bears opened the '40s with an 8-3 record, the same as the year before. But it was good enough to win the Western Division and send the Bears up against the Redskins again for the title. The two teams had met once during the season at Washington, where the Skins prevailed, 7-3. The championship game matched the two great quarterbacks in the league at that time, Sammy Baugh of Washington and Sid Luckman of the Bears. The Bears had painful memories of what Baugh did to them in 1937.

More than 36,000 fans packed the stands at Griffith Stadium on December 8, 1940. This game marked the first time that a pro football game would be broadcast on network radio, so hundreds of thousands of more fans would have the opportunity to hear the game with Red Barber doing the play-by-play.

It was 39 degrees at game time, but the sky was sunny and clear with a slight wind. The Skins marching band played the teams fight song, and the game began at 2:00 p.m. When the dust settled two and a half hours later, the Bears had scored the most points ever in a league championship game or a regular season game, humiliating Washington, 73-0. The halftime score was 28-0, and the Bears just kept piling it on. They amassed 501 yards, 382 rushing and 119 passing. Chicago also picked off eight Washington passes. It was a day that Halas, the Bears, and their fans would not soon forget. On the other side, Skins coach Ray Flaherty and owner George Preston Marshall were left stunned. Halas and the Bears had their revenge.

What made the 1940 Bears so good? One reason was the draft. Chicago was able to acquire running back George McAfee, center Clyde Turner, end Ken Kavanaugh, tackles Lee Artoe and Ed Kolman and halfback Ray "Scooter" McLean. Those rookies plus veterans like Luckman, Fortmann, Stydahar, Musso, Osmanski, and others made the Bears a powerhouse.

Chicago would continue to dominate in the next two seasons. The 1941 team was 10-1, losing only to the Packers at Wrigley Field. Green Bay and Chicago ended up tied at the end of the regular season, so they played a divisional playoff game at Wrigley Field. On December 14, over 43,000 fans saw the Bears cruise to a 33-14 win and a title game shot with the Giants a week later. The Bears were confident but New York came to Chicago and came away with a 37-9 win.

In 1942, it was somewhat of a different Bears team. A number of players joined Uncle Sam. Among those were George McAfee, Ken Kavanaugh, Norm Standlee, Dick Plasman and a few more late in the year. Chicago would also lose the services of George Halas during that season. Lieutenant Commander George Halas of the Naval Reserve would be called to active duty at the age of 47. Halas assigned his coaching duties to assistants Paddy Driscoll, Hunk Anderson and Luke Johnsos.

The Bears went undefeated and untied that year, winning all 11 games, outscoring their opponents, 376-84. They again met the Redskins for the title at Washington. Many observers felt Chicago would have another easy time of it. But the Bears explosive offense was nowhere to be found, and Washington hung on for a 14-10 victory. Just like in 1934, Chicago had registered another unbeaten and untied season, only to lose the championship game. The Bears were only able to score a second quarter touchdown. It was sweet revenge for George Preston Marshall and a hard pill to swallow for Chicago and its Lieutenant Commander George Halas.

What about those years?

1. In the 1940 title game romp over Washington, the Bears scored 11 touchdowns. How many different Bears scored a touchdown?

2. Who scored the first touchdown in that game?

3. Who was the only player to score two touchdowns?

4. How many different Bears scored in that game?

5. How many touchdown passes did Sid Luckman throw?

6. How many passes did the Bears intercept and return for touchdowns?

7. How many times did the Bears punt in the game?

8. Who was the only Bear to kick two extra points?

9. The Bears passed for the extra point after their last two touchdowns. Why?

10. What college did George McAfee attend?

11. What was Clyde Turner's nickname?

12. Where did Turner attend college?

13. In what state is the college that Turner attended located?

14. How many years did Turner play with the Bears and how many times was he named to the Pro Bowl?

15. What position did Turner play on defense?

16. Bears fullback Bill Osmanski had a brother who would join the team in 1946. What was his first name?

17. What position did Osmanski's brother play?

18. During the 1940 season, Sid Luckman set two passing records, for completions and yardage. How many passes did he complete and how many yards did he throw for?

19. Name the Bears who were named to the Pro Bowl after the 1940 season.

20. Besides Washington's 7-3 win over Chicago during the 1940 regular season, who were the two other teams that beat the Bears?

21. In 1941, the Bears beat the College All-Stars. What was the score?

22. On that College All-Star team was a player that had been the Bears' first draft choice that year. However, they were unable to sign him. Who was he?

23. The 1941 Bears averaged how many points per game?

24. What was the lowest point total for the Bears in a single game in 1941?

25. What was the Bears' highest game point total that season?

26. Who did it come against?

27. Who was the Bears' trainer on their 1941 team?

28. Who was named the president of the Bears when Halas left for active duty in WWII?

29. Who led the Bears in scoring in 1942?

Chicago Bears Facts & Trivia

30. How many points did he have?

31. This backup quarterback played two seasons with Chicago. He made his last professional appearance in the 1942 College All-Star Game and threw a touchdown pass. He later went to the Navy and was killed in 1945, the only Bear to die in WWII. Who was he?

32. Who caught his touchdown pass in the College All-Star Game?

33. The 1942 Bears shut out which team twice?

34. Who set a Chicago record for interceptions in 1942?

35. How many did he intercept?

36. Who was the Bears' fullback who was selected a pro bowler in 1942?

37. How many yards did he gain?

38. Who scored the Bears' only touchdown in the 1942 championship game against Washington?

39. What position did he play?

40. This Bear had a touchdown called back in the 1942 title game. Who was he?

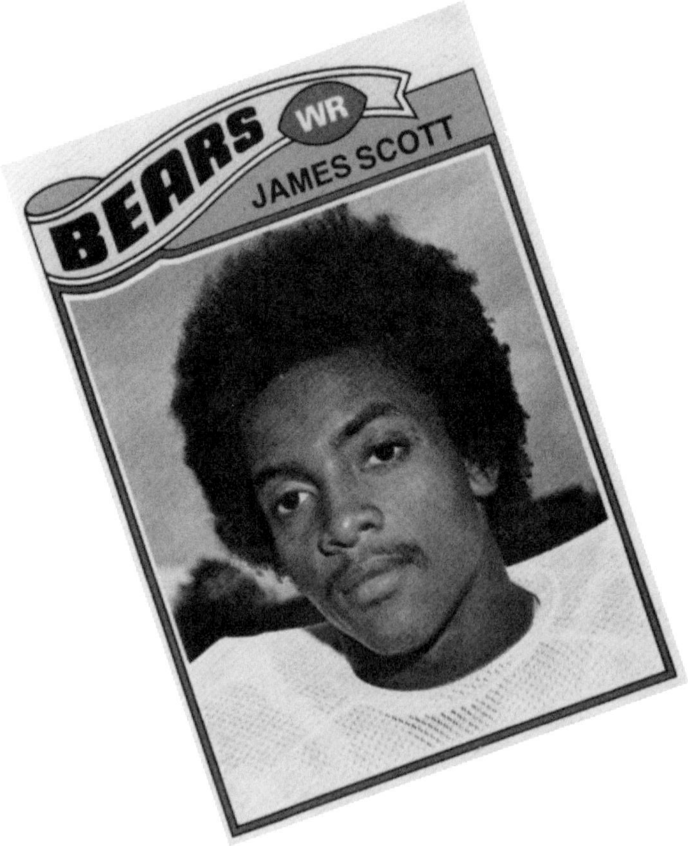
BEARS
WR
JAMES SCOTT

6
Hunk, Luke, and Paddy, But No Papa Bear: 1943-45

With George Halas serving his country in the United States Navy, Hunk Anderson, Luke Johnsos, and Paddy Driscoll were named co-coaches during the 1942 season. When they assembled the following year's team, more Bears were gone. Every other team in the league also lost players, so much so, that the league was reduced to eight teams.

The depletion of talent forced Chicago to seek the services of the retired Bronko Nagurski. The nearly 38-year-old Nagurski had decided to call it quits after the 1937 season but was talked into coming back in 1943. There would be a change though. This time Bronko would not be running the ball. Instead, he would play tackle.

The Bears played a 10-game schedule that year. After tying the Packers in the opener in Green Bay, Chicago won its next seven games before losing to Washington on the road. The last game of the season was against the Bears' crosstown rivals, the Cardinals. If the Bears won, they would clinch the divisional title. If they didn't, a divisional playoff game with Green Bay would have to be played. The Cardinals were 0-9 going into the game, but they didn't play like the worst team in the league and led the Bears, 24-14, at the end of three quarters. The Bears needed help, and they got it from an aging legend. Bronko Nagurski was back running the football, and he keyed a fourth quarter comeback that saw the Bears score 21 points and pull away from the Cardinals, 35-24.

Chicago was now making its fourth straight championship appearance, and it was against their bitter rivals, the Redskins. But on this day, the Skins were no match for the fired up Bears, who walked away with a 41-21 win. Sid Luckman threw five touchdown passes and Bronko Nagurski scored the final touchdown of his career. He retired for good this time.

In 1944, the war had bitten deeper into the Bears roster. Chicago lost 19 of its 28 players from the previous season. Once again, the Bears looked to the past and brought back 35-year-old Gene Ronzani and 37- year-old Carl Brumbaugh. Ronzani was used as a backup for Luckman who had been called to active duty in the Merchant Marine. However, Luckman was able to join his teammates on Sunday, even though he was not able to practice with them during the week. As it turned out, Brumbaugh came to training camp but then decided not to play in the regular season.

In 1944, the Bears finished 6-3-1, second behind the Packers in the Western Division.

The following year the war came to an end. However, many of the Bears' players, including their coach, George Halas, had still not been discharged from the service. So Chicago struggled through its first eight games, winning just one. Finally, with two games left, Halas and most of his players were back. Chicago won its last two games to finish 3-7, the team's worst record ever.

What about those years?

1. Late in the 1943 season, quarterback Sid Luckman set two passing records in a game at the Polo Grounds against the Giants. Name them.

2. How many touchdown passes did Luckman throw that season?

3. How many yards did he throw for?

4. In the 1943 championship game, won by the Bears, 41-21, over the Redskins, Luckman threw five touchdown passes. Who caught them and how many did each catch?

Chicago Bears Facts & Trivia

5. In 1943, Lieutenant Commander George Halas would be shipped to the Pacific Theater of Operations, where he would serve for the rest of the war. What was his job?

6. Whose command did he serve under?

7. How much did each Bear receive for winning the 1943 title?

8. In 1944, the Bears moved their training camp to what location?

9. How many years did they train there?

10. In 1944, Chicago added a player at guard who would later gain fame as an end. Who was he?

11. How many years did he play with the Bears?

12. What college did he play at?

13. What other Bear had played there?

14. Who was the Bears' first round draft pick in 1943?

15. What pick was he overall in the draft?

16. What college did he attend?

17. Who started at right tackle in the 1943 championship game against Washington?

18. Who started at left tackle?

19. What three teams did the Bears beat in 1945?

20. How are all three games similar?

21. This Bear scored three touchdowns after returning from the military in late 1945. He scored them in only 12 minutes of play. Who was he?

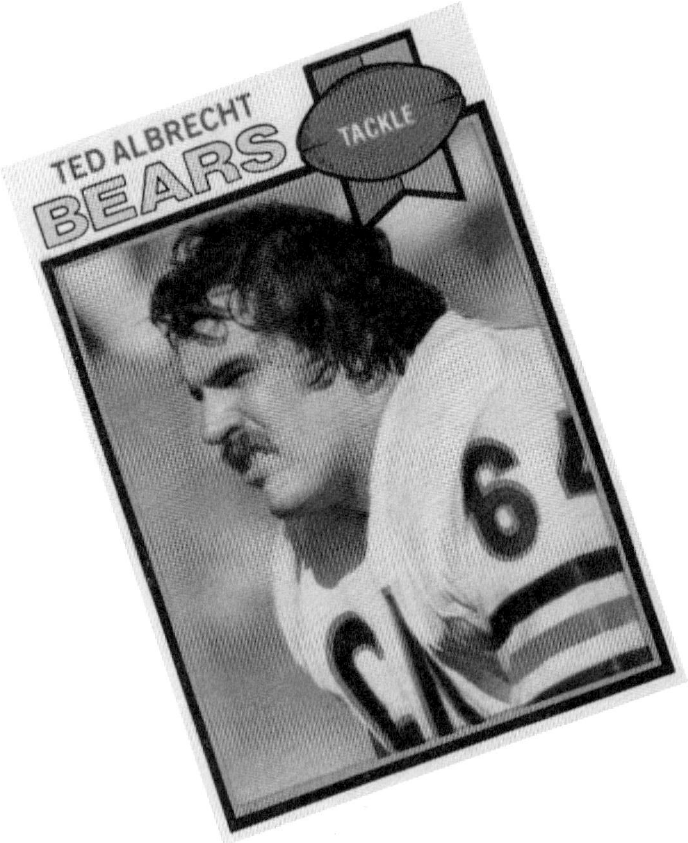
TED ALBRECHT
BEARS
TACKLE
64

7
Climbing Back: 1946-50

In 1946, George Halas was back coaching the Bears. He was now 51 years old, and there were some changes in professional football. For one, a new league had been organized. The All-America Football Conference was the brain-child of Chicago *Tribune* Sports Editor, Arch Ward, who had also started the College All-Star Game. 1946 would be the leagues first season, and it had eight teams including a team from the Windy City, the Chicago Rockets.

Like other teams in the NFL, the Bears were hurt by the new league. Chicago lost fullback Norm Standlee to the San Francisco 49ers, tackle Lee Artoe and halfback Harry Clark to the Los Angeles Dons, and another halfback, Edgar Jones, to the Cleveland Browns.

One of the greatest coaches of all time, Hall-of-Famer, Paul Brown, was the Browns' coach, and he had such players as Otto Graham, Bill Willis, and Lou Groza. Other top names around the new league were Elroy "Crazy Legs" Hirsch, "Wee Willie" Wilkin, and Bob Hoernschmeyer, who played with the Rockets; Ace Parker and Bob Masterson with the New York Yankees along with former Redskins coach Ray Flaherty; Bruno Banducci with the 49ers; and Glenn Dobbs and Dub Jones with the Brooklyn Dodgers. And there were many more.

The new league promised lucrative contracts, and George Halas had to pay his stars more money or lose them. Halas met the salary demands of three of his top players, Luckman, McAfee, and Turner.

Despite all the distractions, Halas was able to field a very solid team in 1946. Joe Stydahar, Hugh Gallarneau, Ken Kavanaugh, Ray Bray, and Bill Osmanski were in uniform. Halas also moved Ed

Sprinkle from guard to end. A rookie from Iowa, Jim Keane, joined the Bears and became one of his finest receivers over the next half dozen years. Plus, the Bears were able to obtain the services of rookie tackle Fred Davis, who became a mainstay on the line throughout the rest of the decade. Sid Luckman once again led the league in passing, taking the Bears into the championship game with the Giants at the Polo Grounds.

Some controversy arose the night before the game when reports surfaced that Giants quarterback Frank Filchock and a teammate, fullback Merle Hapes, had been approached by a New York gambler, who offered them $2,500 in cash to throw the game. He also promised to bet $1,000 on the game for each player and to find them off season jobs. Following the report, the gambler was arrested and new league commissioner Bert Bell suspended Hapes from the game. However, Filchock was allowed to play, but was later suspended.

The controversy didn't seem to phase the Bears as they defeated the Giants, 24-14. Luckman threw a touchdown pass and also ran for one. The defense did its job, and Chicago had another championship.

The 1947 season started out badly for Chicago. The Bears opened with a loss to the Packers in Green Bay and followed that up with a loss to the Cardinals at Comiskey Park. But that seemed to wake the Bears up, and they went on a tear, winning their next eight games before falling to the Rams and once again losing to the Cardinals in the season finale at Wrigley Field, 30-21. That was a costly loss for the Bears because it meant losing the division title. What's more, this was the first time since 1922 that the Cardinals had defeated the Bears in the same season, and the victories helped the Cards win their first division title. The Cardinals then beat the Philadelphia Eagles for their first league title since 1924.

Sid Luckman had another productive year in 1947, completing 196 passes, the second most in the league, for over 2,700 yards. The passing game had certainly come a long was and was now a very potent weapon for most teams. Chicago piled up 363 points, averaging 30.3 points per game, best in the league, and placed three players in the Pro Bowl. But for George Halas and company, the season was not complete.

By the time 1948 rolled around, veterans like Hugh Gallarneau, Bill Osmanski, and Scooter McLean had retired. But Halas had a very successful draft, picking up quarterback Johnny Lujack, lineman

George Connor, and another quarterback named Bobby Layne. Even though Luckman was only 31, Halas was looking to the future when he signed Layne and Lujack.

Luckman started the year at quarterback, and the Bears got off to a quick start, winning their first four games, including a 28-27 win over those pesky Cardinals at Comiskey Park. Then after a 12-7 loss to the Eagles, Chicago won its next six games before coming up against the Cardinals in the season finale. Both teams were 10-1, and the victor would win the division. The game was played in the "friendly confines of Wrigley Field", and it appeared that was the case as the Bears, led by Johnny Lujack, were up, 14-3, at the half. They extended their lead to 21-10 early in the fourth quarter, and it appeared as if the Bears would win. But reserve quarterback Ray Mallouf came off the bench, replacing Paul Christman, and in the last six minutes sparked the Cardinals to two touchdowns and a 24-21 win. Once again it was just like the game before. The Bears seemed jinxed by their cross town rivals.

In 1949, Halas was forced to insert Lujack at quarterback because Luckman was suffering from a thyroid condition. The Bears had already sold Bobby Layne to the New York Bulldogs for a reported $50,000 and two draft choices. To replace Layne at third string quarterback, Halas drafted George Blanda.

Lujack had a great year, leading the league in touchdowns, passing yardage, and completions. He also had his finest day as a pro when he passed for a record 468 yards against the Cardinals. The Bears even won this time in a 52-21 romp. Also in that game, Lujack threw for six touchdowns, just one short of Luckman's record. Despite all of the Bears' offensive exploits, Chicago was just 3-3 after the first six games. Two of those losses came at the hands of a new league powerhouse, the Rams. However, the Bears managed to win their last six games, including that record setting performance by Lujack, and finished 9-3.

By the close of 1949, the All-America Football Conference merged with the NFL as three of its teams, the Cleveland Browns, San Francisco 49ers, and Baltimore Colts, became members of the older league now known as the National-American Football League. The NAFL now had 13 teams. The Colts would be in the National Conference with the Bears and five other teams, and the American Conference would have six teams.

Because of the demise of the AAC, a special draft was held for its players. The NAFL now had a lot of excess, so the league reinstated a rule allowing free substitutions. The "two-way" player was almost extinct as the two platoon system was born.

The Bears had a good draft in 1950 and were 8-2 with a half game lead over the Rams as they entered the next to last game of the season. Chicago had already beaten Los Angeles twice but now had to go up against you know who. The Cardinals had good players that season, but under new head coach Curly Lambeau, they were just 4-6 and in last place in the American Conference. But it never seemed to make any difference as the Cardinals downed the Bears, 20-10, at Comiskey Park to drop the Bears into a tie with the Rams for the National Conference title. Both teams closed out the regular season with wins, which set up a playoff game in Los Angeles, which LA won, 24-14. Chicago had a 7-3 in the second quarter before Bob Waterfield replaced an ineffective Norm Van Brocklin. Waterfield threw two touchdown passes, and the Rams took a 17-7 halftime lead, from which the Bears were unable to recover. The Rams went on to lose the title game to the Browns, 30-28.

Johnny Lujack played with a shoulder injury in 1950 and was obviously not as effective as the year before. An era had ended for Chicago, one which was very successful during the regular season, but one which produced only one championship. The team would decline over the next few years, and there would be a long dry spell before the Bears won another championship.

What about those years?

1. In 1946, Sid Luckman threw one less touchdown pass than league leader Bob Waterfield of the Rams. How many did Luckman throw?

2. What Bear intercepted a pass in the 1946 championship game and ran it back for a touchdown?

3. How many yards did the play cover?

4. This Bear led the league in receptions in 1947. Who was he?

5. How many catches did he have?
6. For how many yards?
7. How many touchdowns did he score?
8. How many touchdown passes did Ken Kavanaugh catch in 1947?
9. How many extra points did Scooter McLean kick that year?
10. How many Bears were Pro Bowlers in 1947?
11. Who were they?
12. George Connor attended two colleges. Which were they?
13. How many years did he play with the Bears?
14. How many times was he voted a Pro Bowler?
15. What year was Connor inducted in the Pro Football Hall of Fame?
16. What distinction did he have in being selected to the Pro Bowl?
17. Backup quarterback Johnny Lujack intercepted how many passes in 1948?
18. Lujack also did the placekicking that season. He converted 44 times. How many did he miss?
19. The largest crowd ever to see a regular season game saw the Bears play what team?
20. Where was the game played?
21. What was the Bears' first television show called?

22. Name the call letters of the television station.

23. What Chicago television channel was it on?

24. Quarterback George Blanda joined the Bears in 1949. What college did he attend?

25. How many points did Blanda score as a Bear?

26. How many field goals did he kick?

27. How many rushing touchdowns did he score?

28. Blanda still holds a Bears record by scoring points in how many consecutive games?

29. Name the next two players on that list and their consecutive game totals.

30. Halfback Jim Canady played how many years with the Bears?

31. What year did he break in?

32. What college did he attend?

33. Tight end Jim Keane tied a league record by catching how many passes in a single game in 1949?

34. How many yards did he gain in that game?

35. How tall was Jim Keane and how much did he weigh?

36. The Bears drafted Jim Morrison from Ohio State in 1950. What was his nickname?

37. What position did he play?

38. How many years did he play with the Bears?

39. This player was a guard who was picked up in 1950 by the Bears after playing with the Baltimore Colts of the AAC. Who was he?

40. What college did he attend?

41. How long did he play for the Bears?

42. The Bears had a halfback in the late 1940s and early 1950s with a first name of Julie. What was his last name?

43. What position did he play?

44. What college did he go to?

45. What number did Johnny Lujack wear as a Bear?

46. This Bears' halfback scored Chicago's first touchdown in the 1950 Western Division playoff game against the Rams. Who was he?

47. How did he score the touchdown?

48. How many yards did the play cover?

49. Who was the Bears leading rusher in 1950?

50. How many yards did he get?

51. How many Bears were selected to play in the 1950 Pro Bowl, which now pitted two teams made up of all-stars from both divisions playing each other, instead of the league champion playing a team of all stars from both divisions?

52. Name them.

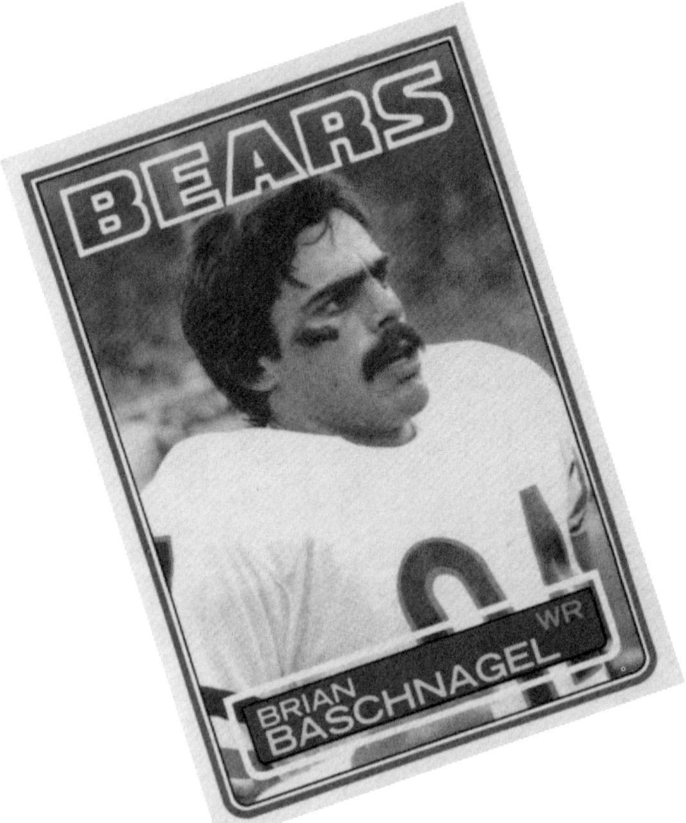
BEARS
WR
BRIAN
BASCHNAGEL

8
Struggling: 1951-57

In 1951, Chicago started off well, winning five of its first six games, but then lost four of their final six to finish 7-5, including another frustrating loss to the Cardinals, which cost the Bears a playoff with LA.

Looking back, Chicago began the season without such stars as Sid Luckman, George McAfee, and Ken Kavanaugh, who had retired. Assistant coach Hunk Anderson was also gone. Anderson had been offered the head coaching job with the Redskins, but Halas would not release him from his Bear contract unless Redskins owner George Preston Marshall gave Chicago their star tackle, Paul Lipscomb. The deal fell through, and Anderson left football.

After the '51 season, Johnny Lujack retired. Despite having a sore shoulder, he led the Bears in total points scored, touchdown passes, passing yardage, and rushing touchdowns. After the season, George Connor and Dick Barwegan were selected to the Pro Bowl.

In 1952, the Bears' quarterbacking duties were shared by George Blanda and Steve Romanik. In the college draft, an end/flanker by the name of Jim Dooley from Miami University was the Bears' first choice. The Bears also took linebacker and future Hall-of-Famer Bill George. Chicago's second choice in the draft was Eddie Macon, who became the first African-American to play for the Bears.

The '52 season was one to forget as Chicago stumbled to a 5-7 record. The only bright spot was a last second victory over the Lions. The Bears finished ahead of only the Dallas Texans, who incidentally picked up their lone win of the season over the Bears.

In 1953, the Bears dropped even lower, finishing 3-8-1. Until that season, Chicago had only lost eight games once, and that was in 1929. The big highlight was a 24-21 win over the Rams, knocking them out of the National Conference title race, which could be taken as kind of a payback for the years Los Angeles had knocked the Bears out of contention. The Lions won their second straight championship with a former Bear by the name of Bobby Layne barking out the plays. Quarterback George Blanda, in what turned out to be his only full year as Chicago's starting quarterback, led the league with 169 pass completions in 362 attempts. He also threw 24 interceptions.

In 1954, the Bears returned to respectability, finishing with a mark of 8-4. They had two quarterbacks, Zeke Bratkowski and Ed Brown., and their top receiver was Harlon Hill. The Bears also picked up tackle Stan Jones, center Larry Strickland, and defensive end Ed Meadows.

The league enacted a new rule prior to the season which required all players to wear face masks. It prompted one writer to say that it was "no longer possible to determine the quality of a player by the number of teeth he was missing."

After an opening day drubbing by Bobby Layne and the World Champion Lions in Detroit, 48-23, the Bears traveled to Green Bay, where they beat the Packers, 10-3. The following week they beat the Colts at Wrigley Field, but followed that up with a loss at home against the 49ers. The next week they lost in LA and eventually finished 8-4.

One of the most exciting endings in Bears' history occurred during the '54 season. Chicago was playing the 49ers in Kezar Stadium. With about 45 seconds left in the game, San Francisco kicked a field goal to take a 27-24 lead and an apparent victory. But the Bears' Ed Sprinkle took the kickoff and stepped out of bounds to stop the clock. There were 35 seconds left. The 49ers knew the Bears would pass to their prize rookie, Harlon Hill, who had already caught three touchdown passes that day. Darkness was closing in, and on the first play, quarterback George Blanda pitched out to Ed Brown, who had lined up at halfback. Brown started on an end run, but then turned, dropped back, and launched a 40-yard pass to Hill who never broke stride as he raced down the sideline to the end zone for the winning score in a 31-27 win. For the season, Hill led the league in touchdown catches with 12. His 45 receptions were good for 1,124 yards, a 25 yard average per catch. He broke Jim Keane's pass yardage record of 910 yards, set seven years earlier. Hill was the only Bear named to the Pro Bowl.

When 1955 rolled around, George Halas announced that he would retire at the end of season. He was now 60 years old. Up to that time, the Bears had won seven championships, eight division titles, along with one division tie. That was more than any other team. Going into the season, Halas thought he had the makings of another championship team. He had picked up defensive end Doug Atkins from Cleveland. Atkins was 6'8" and weighed 255 pounds. Fullback Rick Casares was drafted from Florida, halfback Bobby Watkins came to Chicago via Ohio State, and linebacker Joe Fortunato came from Mississippi State. One of the Bears quarterbacks, Zeke Bratkowski, went to the service, but Halas regained the services of Bob Williams, who had just been released from the Navy. George Blanda was still suffering the effects of a shoulder injury sustained the year before. Halas only used him as a placekicker. Ed Brown was given the starting quarterback job.

After losing their first three games, the Bears won eight of their last nine games, to finish at 8-4. The Rams won the division with an 8-3-1 record. The stoppers for the Bears once again were the Cardinals. The Bears brought a six-game winning streak into Comiskey Park against their 3-5-1 opponents, but they lost in a blizzard, 53-14.

Despite the loss, the Bears had made it back to being a serious contender. Quarterback Ed Brown completed 52 percent of his passes that year, and his two ends, Harlon Hill and Bill McColl, had good seasons. Rookie fullback Rick Casares rushed for 672 yards and led the league with 5.4 yards a carry. The Bears had eight players named to the Pro Bowl.

In 1956, Paddy Driscoll succeeded Halas as head coach. Chicago lost is first game to the Colts, 28-21, in Baltimore, before going on a seven game winning streak. After a tie with the Giants, the Bears were routed by the Lions, 42-10, in Detroit. But the team regrouped and won the divisional championship with a 10-3 win over the Cardinals and completed the regular season with a 38-21 win over the Lions. Chicago finished the year at 9-2-1 to win their division, but the Bears were routed by the Giants in the championship game, 47-7.

Hope was high for the 1957 season, but the Bears stumbled out of the gate, losing their first two games on the road and the third game at home, before beating the Rams at Wrigley Field, 34-26. The Bears continued to play up and down and finished the season at 5-7. There were few bright spots for Chicago. Fullback Rick Casares had a respectable year, finishing second in the league in rushing behind Cleveland's Jim Brown. However, quarterback Ed Brown completed just 45 percent of his passes. Star receiver Harlon Hill was injured for much of the season and only caught 21 passes. The Bears' defense played well, giving up fewer points than the 9-2-1 team of 1956. But it did not receive any help from the offense.

What about those years?

1. What was "Kayo" Dottley's first name?

2. Dottley was the Bears leading rusher in 1951. How many yards did he have?

3. What college did he attend?

4. How many years did Babe Dimancheff play with the Bears?

5. What team did he spend most of his career with?

6. What was Babe's real first name?

7. What position did he play?

8. How many years did Jim Dooley play with the Bears?

9. Eddie Macon was the first black to play on the Bears. What college did he come from?

10. What position did he play?

11. How many carries did he have as a rookie?

12. How many yards did he average per carry as a rookie?

13. How many years did he play with the Bears?

14. What running back led the Bears in rushing in both '52 and '53?

15. What was his best yardage total in those two seasons?
16. What college did Harlon Hill attend?
17. What state was it located in?
18. How many years did Hill play with the Bears?
19. How many 100-yard pass receiving games does he have?
20. How many consecutive 100-yard receiving games does he have?
21. What were the most receiving yards for Hill in one game?
22. On what date did that occur?
23. How many years Hill gain over 1,000 yards receiving?
24. What were the most 100-yard receiving games for Hill in a season?
25. What year did it happen?
26. How many receiving yards did Hill have in his career?
27. How many career touchdowns did he have?
28. What college did J.C. Caroline attend?
29. How many years did he play with the Bears?
30. What other position did he play besides defensive back?
31. How many touchdowns did Caroline have in 1956 from pass interceptions?
32. Who scored the only touchdown for the Bears in the 1956 title game loss to the Giants?

33. How many yards did the Bears as a team gain rushing in 1956?

34. How many rushing touchdowns did they have?

35. How many first downs?

36. How many Bears were named to the Pro Bowl in 1956?

37. Name them.

38. Who was the Bears leading receiver on the 1957 team?

39. How many passes did he catch?

40. How many receiving yards did he have?

41. The Bears lost twice to Baltimore in 1957. Who was the Colts' quarterback?

42. Name the only team Chicago lost to twice in 1957.

43. What Bear running back became a starter in 1957?

44. What college did he attend?

45. How many years was he with the Bears?

46. How many touchdowns did he score for the Bears?

47. How many career rushing yards did he have?

48. How many rushing touchdowns did he have?

49. In 1957, where did the Bears rank in the 12-team league as far as salaries go?

50. What was the salary range for Chicago?

9
Papa Bear Returns Again: 1958-62

After 1957, Papa Bear George Halas decided to return as head coach for a third time. Paddy Driscoll was moved up to the front office and was demoted to an assistant coach on the field. Also hired as assistants were Chuck Mather and George Allen.

In the draft, Chicago picked up wide receiver Johnny Morris. They also picked up veteran guard Abe Gibron from the Eagles.

Ed Brown was still at quarterback and was spelled at times by Zeke Bratkowski. Chicago was hampered by injuries to Hill and Galimore but still got out of the gate quickly in 1958, winning five of its first seven games. After stumbling against the Colts at home, the Bears finished 8-4, tied for second in the conference with the Rams.

1959 started out slowly with an opening day loss to the Packers in Green Bay, 9-6. After losing four of their first five games, the Bears rebounded to win seven in a row and finished once again in second place with another 8-4 mark. However, the Chicago defense improved when linebacker Larry Morris was acquired in a trade and safety Richie Petitbon was drafted. Both would play huge roles in the future for Chicago.

In 1960, a number of things would occur. For one, the American Football League was born. Three previous leagues of the same name had been formed, but this one would survive and eventually lead to a merger with the NFL. Another change had the Cardinals moving from Chicago to St. Louis. And finally, the Dallas Cowboys were admitted to the league, raising the number of teams in the NFL to 13.

Going into the 1960 season, the Bears had a seven-game winning streak, which grew to eight with an opening day win over the Packers. Chicago was bombarded by the Colts the following week, 42-7, but then won two in a row before tying the Rams. After that, the Bears were erratic and finished 5-6-1. Chicago's final two losses were shutouts. The season even included a 41-13 thumping at the hands of the Packers under second year coach Vince Lombardi. It was the first time Green Bay had won in Chicago since 1952.

The '61 Bears needed offense. They had been outscored by over 100 points the previous season, which was punctuated by season ending losses to the Browns, 42-0, and to the Lions, 36-0. Halas picked up veteran quarterback Bill Wade from the Rams and drafted tight end Mike Ditka and center Mike Pyle.

Meanwhile, the NFL added Minnesota to bring the league to 14 teams. It was the Vikings, with rookie quarterback Fran Tarkenton, who beat the Bears in the season opener, 37-13, as Tarkenton threw four touchdown passes. The Bears went on to finish 8-6, good for a third-place tie with the Colts.

Quarterback Bill Wade passed for over 2,000 yards, and Willie Galimore rushed for 707 yards, averaging 4.6 yards a carry. Rookie Mike Ditka made a big impact as he led the Bears receivers with 56 catches, 12 for touchdowns. Also that season, Johnny Morris had been moved from running back to flanker, and he proved to be a threat on long passes. The Bears had a lot of offense, scoring 326 points, but the defense gave up to 302. Still, there was something about the team that was promising.

In 1962, Chicago fulfilled some of that promise, as it started out with road wins over the 49ers and the Rams before being pounded by the Packers in Green Bay, 49-0. After a sluggish mid-season, Chicago won five of its last six games. Included in those victories was a one-point win over the Vikings at home, followed by a one-point victory over the Cowboys in Dallas. Chicago ended the season with a 3-0 win at home over the Lions and finished the year at 9-5. The Bears had some defensive lapses but were showing improvement and had helped themselves by picking up defensive end Ed O'Bradovich in the draft along with defensive back Bennie McRae.

Offensively, Bill Wade set two new team records; most passing yardage with 3,172 and most completions with 225. He also threw 18 touchdowns. Ditka and Morris each had 58 receptions. The passing game had to excel because Casares and Galimore were injured for much of the season. Despite the injuries and the domination of another Western Division foe, the Green Bay Packers, it was a building block season for Chicago.

What about those years?

1. George Halas brought in George Allen as an assistant coach for the 1958 season. What team did Allen come from?

2. What unit did Allen coach with that team?

3. How long did Allen coach with Chicago?

4. After a court dispute that the Bears won over a head coaching position, Allen was offered, Halas released him from his contract. What head coaching job did Allen take over?

5. Flanker Johnny Morris attended what college?

6. How long did he play with Chicago?

7. Morris was a running back and receiver when drafted by the Bears. What other roles did he play for them early in his career?

8. How many passes did Morris catch as a Bear?

9. How many consecutive games did he catch a pass in?

10. What was his highest total for receiving yardage in a season?

11. In what year did that occur?

12. How many 100-yard receiving games did Morris have in his career?

13. What was his best season for 100-yard receiving games?

14. In what year did that happen?

15. What was Morris's highest yardage total for one game?

16. Before joining the Bears in 1958, Morris was a co-holder of what sprint record?

17. What was his time?

18. After his playing career ended, what career did Morris take up?

19. From what NFL team did the Bears get linebacker Larry Morris?

20. What relation is Larry Morris to Johnny Morris?

21. What college did Larry attend?

22. How long did play with the Bears?

23. Who were the three "B's" that quarterbacked the Bears in 1959?

24. How many years did Abe Gibron play with the Bears?

25. What position did he play?

26. What Big Ten school did he attend?

27. How many years did Gibron serve as a Bears assistant coach?

28. How many years was he the head coach?

29. What was his record as head coach?

30. What years did he serve as head coach?

31. What was the only team Gibron was able to beat twice?

32. What college did Roosevelt Taylor attend?

Chicago Bears Facts & Trivia

33. What college did Dave Whitsell attend?

34. This center from Yale joined Chicago in 1961. Who was he?

35. How many years did he play with the Bears?

36. Willie Galimore helped beat the Colts in 1961 when he caught a screen pass and scored. How long was the touchdown?

37. How many years did Bill Wade play with the Bears?

38. What was his completion percentage in 1961?

39. How many times did he pass for 2,000 yards in a season?

40. Who was the other Bear killed along with Willie Galimore in a car accident prior to the 1964 season?

41. How many years was this player with the Bears?

42. Placekicker Roger Leclerc kicked five field goals against what team in 1961?

43. What other position did Leclerc play?

44. How many years did he play with the Bears?

45. What were the most field goal attempts he had in a game?

46. What was lifetime field goal percentage?

47. What Bear was named the 1962 Rookie-of-the-Year?

48. What college did he attend?

49. How many years did he play for the Bears?

50. What number did Ted Karras wear with Chicago?

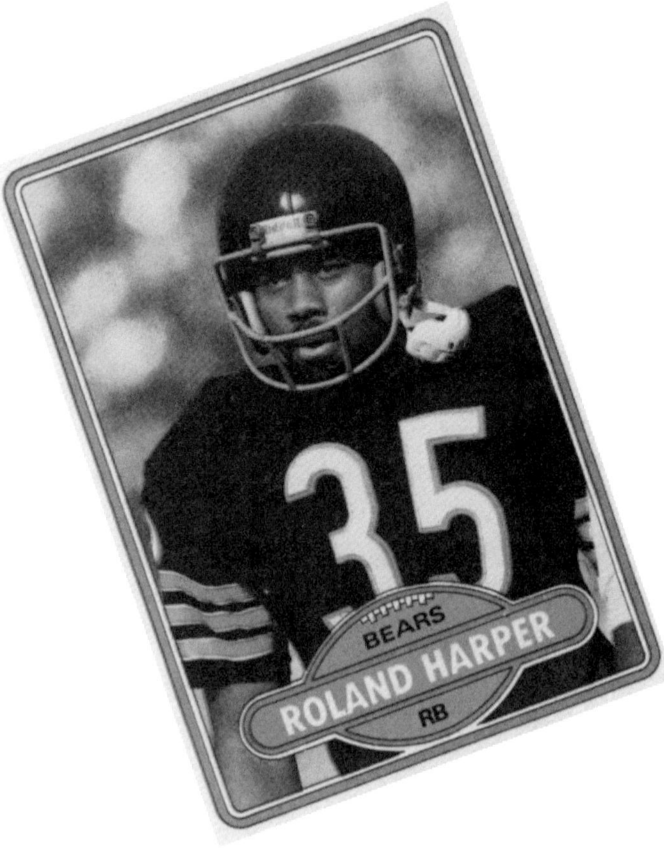
35
BEARS
ROLAND HARPER
RB

10
Champions: 1963

The Bears were on a high entering the '63 season. They ended the previous year by winning five of their last six games, and Halas was encouraged. Still he knew the champion Packers were once again the team to beat.

Halas didn't make any major changes with the exception of moving Stan Jones from offensive guard to defensive tackle. He also added rookie end Bob Jencks, who could also kick extra points, and hired former Bear receiver Jim Dooley as an assistant coach.

Chicago opened the season in Green Bay, against a team that had beaten the Bears, 49-0 and 38-7, the year before. But Chicago stopped the Packers, 10-3, which started them on a five-game winning streak to open the season. Then, the Bears lost to a lowly 49ers team on the road, 20-14, which dropped them into a first place conference tie with Green Bay. But they rebounded to win four in a row, including another win over the Packers, 26-17, in Chicago. Tie games with the Steelers and Vikings followed, but then the Bears took out their revenge on the 49ers with a 26-7 win and closed the regular season with another victory at home, 24-14, over the Lions. Chicago finished 9-1-2, just a half game in front of the Packers, whose only losses came at the hands of the Bears. The Bears earned the right to play the New York Giants for the league championship.

The Giants had won the Eastern Conference for the third straight year and five out of the last six. The were led by 37-year-old quarterback Y.A. Tittle, who almost matched his age in touchdown passes, throwing 36. New York was aging but still had veteran stars in Frank

Gifford, Andy Robustelli, Hugh McElhenny, and Rosey Brown. It was the first championship game at Wrigley Field since 1943, and it was also the first time the Bears were in a championship game, since a loss to, you guessed it, the Giants in 1956. 45,800 fans crammed into Wrigley Field on that December 29. The game time temperature was nine degrees above zero, and the Giants were 10-point favorites. They scored first in the opening quarter on a 14-yard pass from Tittle to Gifford. New York threatened again later in the quarter, but wide receiver Del Shofner dropped a pass in the end zone. Then the Bears defense took over. On the next play, linebacker Larry Morris picked off a Tittle pass and lumbered 61 yards to the Giants' five-yard line. Bill Wade then scored himself from the two. The Giants did come back to take the lead at halftime on a 13-yard field goal from Don Chandler, but the Bears now had some confidence in their defense.

In the third quarter, the defense came up big once again. Ed O'Bradovich intercepted a Tittle screen pass and returned it 10 yards to the Giants' 14. On a crucial third and nine, Wade found Ditka, who nearly scored. Then the quarterback scored once again on the next play. The Bears' Richie Petitbon ended the Giants' final threat with an interception in the closing seconds. On the game's final play, Wade fell on the ball, and Chicago had won its eighth championship. The Giants had outgained the Bears offensively, but the Bears defense came up big when it had to.

What about those years?

1. The 1963 Bears defense led the league in 10 of 19 categories. How many points did Chicago allow per game?

2. How many yards rushing per game did the Bears give up?

3. How many rushing touchdowns were allowed?

4. How many passes did Chicago intercept?

5. What Bear led the league in interceptions?

Chicago Bears Facts & Trivia   65

6. How many did he have?

7. How much money did each Bear receive as his share of the championship game receipts?

8. The 1963 Bears tied two straight games. What were the scores of those games?

9. Who received the championship game ball?

10. How many Bears were named to the 1963 Pro Bowl?

11. Who were they?

12. Who was the Bears' trainer?

13. In 1963, the Pro Football Hall of Fame opened in Canton, Ohio. 17 charter members were enshrined. How many were Bears?

14. Name them.

15. Quarterback Bill Wade scored both touchdowns against the Giants in the title game. How long were the runs?

16. What Bear caught the game's opening kickoff?

17. The 1963 championship game marked the anniversary of what game?

18. Who played in that game?

19. 1963 marked how many years that George Halas had coached the Bears?

20. Tight end Mike Ditka made a dramatic catch and run during the season against Pittsburgh to salvage a tie. How long did the play cover?

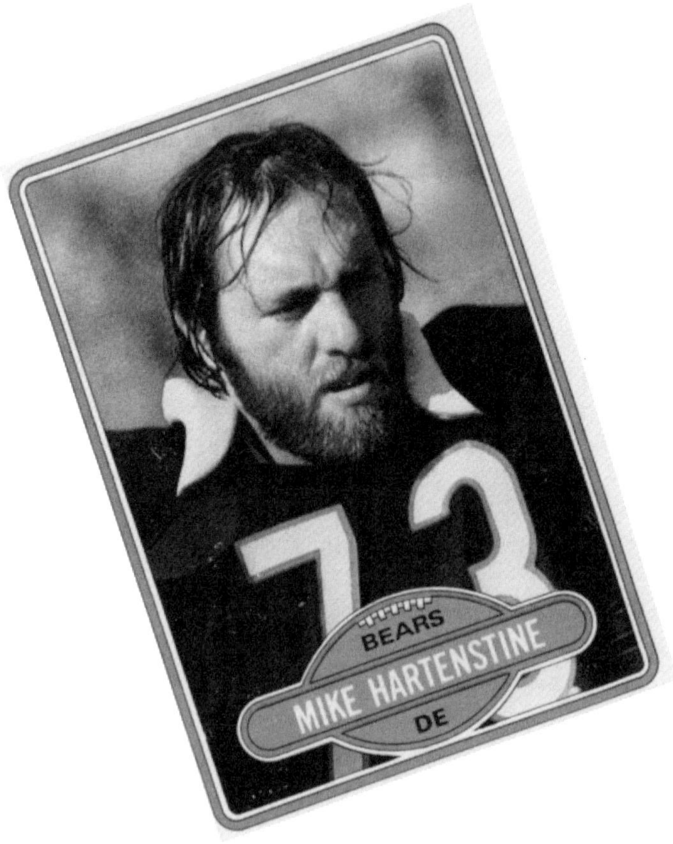
BEARS
MIKE HARTENSTINE
DE

II
Tragedy and Inconsistency: 1964-67

The '63 championship team was dealt a tragic blow in July 1964 when halfback Willie Galimore and end Bo Farrington were killed when their car missed a curve and flipped into a field. They were only a few miles from training camp in Rensselaer, Indiana, attempting to make the 11 p.m. curfew.

That tragic incident set the tone for the season. Injuries to several key players caused the Bears to stumble to a 5-9 record. The league leading defense of a year before suffered the most. Bill George, Doug Atkins, and Ed O'Bradovich missed much of the season, and Larry Morris and Joe Fortunato also missed a few games.

Offensively, without Galimore's running, the Bears went to the air. Wade completed 56 percent of his passes while his running mate, Rudy Bukich, led the league with a 62 percent mark. Their targets were Johnny Morris, who caught 93 passes for 1,200 yards, and Mike Ditka, who snared 75. But not even those numbers could prevent Chicago from slipping into sixth place in the western division.

The Bears needed some new blood, and in the '65 draft, they found it. They came up with two players who would later be elected to the Hall of Fame. They were, of course, Gale Sayers and Dick Butkus. With those two players and others added through acquisitions, Chicago reversed their fortunes of a year before and went 9-5 in 1965.

There were many offensive highlights that year, but none more dramatic than the six-touchdown explosion by Sayers on December 12, on a muddy Wrigley Field, against San Francisco. George Halas said, "It was the greatest performance ever by one man on a football field." 49ers assistant coach Y.A. Tittle reportedly said, "I just wonder how many that Sayers would have scored if we hadn't set our defense to stop him." Of those six touchdowns, four were runs, one came on a screen pass, and the other on a punt return. That tied a league record. The Bears avenged an opening day loss to the 49ers with a 61-20 romp.

Ironically, on that same Sunday, the Packers Paul Hornung scored five touchdowns, but that was lost in the din of Sayers's accomplishment.

Quarterback Rudy Bukich had a good year, completing 56 percent of his passes, and Johnny Morris led the team with 53 catches.

The Bears defense, which took its cues as time went on from the ferocious Butkus, made noticeable improvement over the year before.

Needless to say, Sayers was named the Rookie of the Year.

High hopes were felt in 1966, but Chicago stumbled out of the gate and tripped all the way to a 5-7-2 record, fifth in the conference. The Packers lost only two games, beat the Cowboys for the league championship, then defeated the Kansas City Chiefs in the first Super Bowl.

What caused the Bears' downfall? Injuries were one reason. Another was that some of their top defensive players had left. George had been traded to the Rams, and Larry Morris ended up with the expansion Atlanta Falcons. Offensively, Sayers led the league in rushing with 1,231 yards and set a league record for combined net yardage and was the only Bear named to the Pro Bowl.

Because of the fierce competition for players between the two leagues, the powers to be decided that something had to be done, so a merger was announced in 1966. Starting in 1967, the AFL and the NFL would participate in the college draft together. However, they would play separate schedules until 1970, when the merger would take effect.

Prior to 1967, the now 16-team National Football League was restructured so that each conference had two four-team divisions. The Bears played in the Central Division with their arch rivals, the Packers, along with Detroit and a much improved Minnesota team.

Going into the season, George Halas had a decision to make at quarterback. Billy Wade had retired, and Rudy Bukich was aging. So Halas traded Mike Ditka to the Eagles for back-up quarterback Jack Concannon. Halas made some other trades, including sending Doug Atkins and Herman Lee to the expansion New Orleans Saints for

Chicago Bears Facts & Trivia

offensive guard Don Croftcheck.

That year Chicago finished 7-6-1, second in the Central Division behind the Packers, who went on to win their second-straight Super Bowl. Gale Sayers, despite being hampered by an ankle injury, still gained 1,689 all purpose yards, but dropped to third in the league in rushing. Butkus, by now, was the most intimidating linebacker in the league, and he and Sayers were selected to the Pro Bowl. A problem area remained at quarterback. Jack Concannon completed only 49 percent of his passes. At the end of the season, Halas, who was nearing his 73rd birthday, had plenty to think about.

What about those years?

1. In 1964, the Bears picked up a defensive lineman from Tennessee. Who was he?

2. How many years did he play with them?

3. What position did Jon Arnett play?

4. Arnett led the Bears in rushing in 1964, with how many yards?

5. How was he acquired by the Bears?

6. How many years did he play with Chicago?

7. What college did Andy Livingston attend?

8. How many seasons did he play for the Bears?

9. What college did Larry Rakestraw attend?

10. What position did he play?

11. How many years was he with Chicago?

12. The Bears had three first-round draft selections in 1965. Besides

Sayers and Butkus, who was the other player selected?

13. What happened with that player?

14. What college was Dick Gordon drafted from?

15. How long did he play with the Bears?

16. What position did Ralph Kurek play?

17. What college did he attend?

18. How long did he play with Chicago?

19. What college did Brian Piccolo attend?

20. What former Bear was his first college coach?

21. How many years was Piccolo with the Bears?

22. What disease ended his career and his life?

23. What position did Rudy Kuechenberg play?

24. What college was he drafted from?

25. How many years did he play with the Bears?

26. In what year was he drafted?

27. How many passes did Rudy Bukich have intercepted in 1965?

28. How many passes did he throw?

12
A New Era: 1968-73

An era ended for good in 1968. On May 27, George Halas announced that he was retiring for the last time. The 73-year-old "Papa Bear" said he made the decision with no regrets, even though it was very difficult. He told those assembled that, "I knew it was time to quit when I was chewing out an official and he walked off the penalty faster than I could keep up with him." Vintage Halas.

Another legendary coach, Vince Lombardi, also gave up the reins in Green Bay that year although he would come back later to coach the Redskins for one year.

On May 28, Bears assistant coach Jim Dooley was named the new head coach. The 38-year-old Dooley had spent nine seasons as an end for the Bears and had been an assistant coach for five years.

After winning four of five pre-season games, Chicago dropped its first two regular season contests before Dooley won his first game as coach, 27-17, over the Vikings at Minnesota. The Bears were 7-6 going into the last game of the season, at home, against the Packers. A win would give the Bears the Central Division title over Minnesota. However, the Bears, despite two fourth-quarter touchdowns, lost a heartbreaker to Green Bay, 28-27.

Besides losing the game and not making the playoffs, Chicago had suffered another crushing blow when Gale Sayers suffered a serious knee injury on November 10 and was lost for the season.

Also, in the third game of the season at Minnesota, quarterback Jack Concannon left the game with a broken collarbone. Then backup Rudy Bukich cam in and suffered a shoulder separation and was through for the season. Larry Rakestraw finished the game and started the next two before being benched in favor of Virgil Carter. Concannon was finally able to return in the 12th game of the season. So, it was a very tough year, but Chicago was still optimistic because Sayers would be back and they still had a healthy Butkus. Once again Butkus and Sayers were named to the Pro Bowl.

1969 started slow with four straight losses. Jack Concannon was benched in favor of rookie Bobby Douglas. But after three games, Virgil Carter was given the job. He was able to lead the Bears to a 38-7 win over the 1-6 Steelers, but that proved to be the only victory for Chicago all season. Both Pittsburgh and the Bears ended with the worst record in the league at 1-13. But because the Bears beat the Steelers, Pittsburgh received the first choice in draft. That first pick would change Pittsburgh's destiny in a few years, for he was a quarterback from Louisiana Tech by the name of Terry Bradshaw. Ah, the luck of the draw!

The lone bright spot in 1969 was the return of Gale Sayers. Even though he would never again be the same runner he was before his knee injury, he did lead the league in rushing with 1,032 yards.

In 1970, after the worst year in their history, the Bears could only go up, and they did, finishing 6-8. But Chicago received more tragic news before the season when running back Brian Piccolo died of cancer at the age of 26.

Dooley used Concannon at quarterback, and he led the team to wins in the first two weeks of the season. But then Sayers suffered another knee injury and was lost for the year. Concannon was replaced by Douglas, who was promptly injured and also lost for the season, so Concannon was back as the starter. The December 13 win over the Packers, 35-17, was historic because it was the last game the Bears played in Wrigley Field. The Bears ended up finishing third. Dick Gordon had a big year, leading the league in receptions with 71 and TD catches with 13, and he and Butkus were named to the Pro Bowl.

In 1971, the Bears, in their new home at Soldier Field, won five of their first seven games but then faltered to finish 6-8. In the last five games, the offense scored just 29 points.

1971 marked the end of the short but brilliant career of Gale Sayers. He had been unable to return from nagging knee injuries and carried the ball just 13 times for 38 yards.

The quarterback woes continued for Coach Dooley. Kent Nix was

Chicago Bears Facts & Trivia

at the helm for most of the first half of the season but completed only 37 percent of his passes. Bobby Douglas took over, and though he ran well, he completed only 40 percent of his passes.

After the season, Halas fired Dooley and named former Bear player and assistant coach Abe Gibron to succeed him.

The Bears had a good draft in 1972 but went nowhere during the season. After the first four games, the Bears had lost three and tied one. Later, they managed a three-game winning streak over the Browns, Vikings, and Cardinals, but there were few other highlights during the season. Bobby Douglas had a great year running the ball, picking up 968 yards, but he completed just 38 percent of his passes. Chicago led the conference in rushing with 2,360 yards, but they were anemic at putting points on the board.

In 1973, The Bears sunk even lower to 3-11. There was still no passing game, so Gibron replaced Douglas in the 10th game of the season with rookie Gary Huff, who promptly threw four interceptions against the Lions. The Bears finished in the cellar for the second year in a row. It had now been five long years without a winning season, the worst period in the Bears' storied history.

What about those years?

1. What was Jim Dooley's coaching record with the Bears?

2. This former Bear, who was in the Hall of Fame, was still an assistant coach until he died in the summer of 1968. Name him.

3. Who was the Bears' first draft choice in 1968?

4. What position did he play?

5. What college did he come from?

6. How many times did he carry the ball and how many yards did he gain his rookie season?

7. This player, who would eventually replace Gale Sayers returning

kickoffs, was drafted in 1968. Who was he?

8. What other position did he play?

9. What college did he attend?

10. Gale Sayers set a rushing record with 205 yards against what team in 1968?

11. Who won the game?

12. What was the score?

13. Where was the game played?

14. Mac Percival led the league in 1968 with how many field goals?

15. Percival did not miss an extra point. How many did he have that year?

16. The Bears finished 7-7 in 1968. How many teams in the league had worse records?

17. What college did Bobby Douglas attend?

18. What was his lifetime average per rushing attempt?

19. What was his highest rushing average in a season?

20. How many rushing touchdowns did he have in 1972?

21. How many career touchdowns did he have with the Bears?

22. How many years did Douglas lead the Bears in rushing?

23. In 1972, Douglas recovered how many Bear fumbles?

24. What was his career passing completion percentage as a Bear?

25. What was his average gain per pass?
26. How many touchdown passes did he throw?
27. What was his quarterback rating as a Bear?
28. How many interceptions did he throw with Chicago?
29. How many years did Douglas play with the Bears?
30. Bears' quarterback Virgil Carter was traded to what team?
31. After what season?
32. The 1967 Bears averaged how many points on offense?
33. How many points did they give up per game?
34. How many times were the Bears shut out in 1969?
35. The Bears acquired three Packers in 1970. Who were they?
36. What was Jack Concannon's nickname?
37. What team did Craig Baynham play for before he came to the Bears?
38. How long did he play for Chicago?
39. George Farmer attended what college?
40. What position did he play?
41. How many kickoffs did Cecil Turner return for touchdowns in 1970?
42. How many yards did he average per return?
43. Who led the Bears in rushing in 1970?

44. What was his total?

45. What college was Joe Moore drafted from?

46. What year was he drafted?

47. How long was he a Bear?

48. Cyril Pinder was acquired from what team?

49. How long did he play with Bears?

50. What position did he play?

51. Where did quarterback Kent Nix attend college?

52. In a 16-15 win over the Redskins in 1971, the extra point on the final Bear touchdown was scored in an unusual way. What happened?

53. Abe Gibron played two seasons with the Bears. How long did he play in the NFL?

54. What other teams did he play for and for how long?

55. What Bear led the league in kickoff returns in 1972?

56. What was his average return?

57. Wally Chamberlain attended what college?

58. What round was he drafted in?

59. What year was he drafted?

60. What position did he play?

61. How long was he a Bear?

Chicago Bears Facts & Trivia

62. What position did Allan Ellis play?

63. What round was quarterback Gary Huff drafted in?

64. What team did Carl Garrett play for before coming to the Bears?

65. Who were the Bears radio voices on WGN from 1953-76?

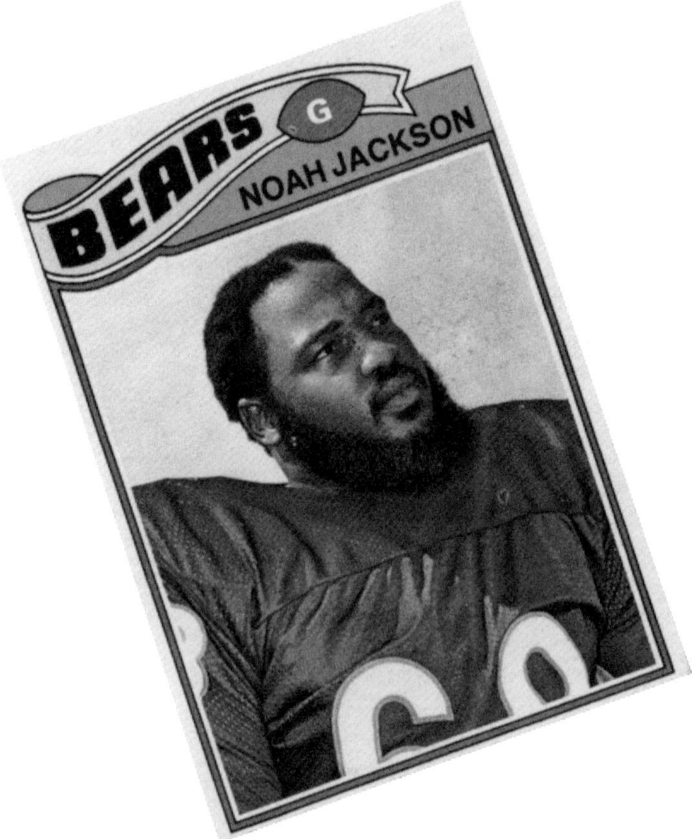
BEARS
G
NOAH JACKSON

13
And Along Came Sweetness: 1974-81

George Halas was not accustomed to losing, and after five-straight losing seasons, he wanted desperately to get the Bears winning again.

On September 12, 1974, Jim Finks was hired as the Bears' general manager, vice-president, and chief operating officer. Finks had become general manager of the Vikings in 1964, and he had helped turn that team into a powerhouse, winning five division titles and going to the Super Bowl twice under his reign. Halas believed, if anyone could turn his team around, it was Finks.

But it would take time. The '74 team finished 4-10, losing seven of its last eight games. After the season, Abe Gibron was fired as head coach, and Jack Pardee succeeded him.

In the '75 draft, the Bears' first choice was an unheralded running back from Jackson State College named Walter Payton. Finks was beginning to build his own team, and as it turned out, it was quite a way to start, with Walter Payton. Also that year, Finks added quarterback Bob Avellini, running back Roland Harper, defensive end Mike Hartenstine, center Dan Peiffer, and kicker Bob Thomas.

The '75 Bears once again struggled, finishing 4-10. Bob Avellini took over at quarterback late in the season, and the Bears won two of their last three games. Walter Payton had a fairly productive first season with 679 yards rushing. He only averaged 3.5 yards per rush, but he did manage 134 yards on 25 carries and 300 net yards in the last game of the season against the Saints. The defense also struggled, giving up 379 points, the most in the NFC.

Chicago had a good draft in 1976, adding wide receivers James Scott and Brian Baschnagel and safety Gary Fencik. Chicago won three of its first four games and finished the season at 7-7, the first time in eight years the Bears had a .500 season. Walter Payton had a big year, leading the NFC in rushing with 1,390 yards and finished second in the league behind O.J. Simpson. Payton also tied Minnesota's Chuck Foreman for the most rushing touchdowns in the NFC with 13. Avellini had some problems at quarterback as he completed only 44 percent of his passes. Payton and Wally Chambers were named to the Pro Bowl, and Pardee was named NFC Coach of the Year. There was a lot of promise on the horizon.

Expectations were high in 1977, but the Bears started slowly, losing four of their first seven games, including a 47-0 pasting by the Oilers at the Astrodome. The following week Chicago won a come-from-behind thriller over the Chiefs, after trailing, 17-0, at halftime. Payton rushed for 192 yards in that game. That win jump-started the Bears. The following week against Minnesota Payton set a league single-game rushing record of 275 yards. Chicago would run off a six-game winning streak, the final victory, a 12-9 win over the Giants in New York on a field covered with slush and snow. It was reminiscent of the 1934 "Sneakers Game" and the 1956 title game, both against the Giants. Bob Thomas finally nailed a 27-yard field goal with 12 seconds left in overtime for the Bears' first ever overtime win, and it secured a playoff berth for Chicago.

In the playoffs, Chicago was no match for Dallas, as the eventual Super Bowl champs, cruised, 37-7. But good things were happening. The offense, led by Walter Payton, was starting to jell. Walter set three league records and 13 team records in 1977 and was named NFL MVP.

But amid all the success, coach Jack Pardee resigned after the season to take the head coaching job with the Redskins, and Neil Armstrong was hired as his replacement. It was not a good time for a coaching resignation, and the repercussions were felt the next year.

When 1978 rolled around, the Bears felt their nucleus was solid, despite the distraction of a new head coach and a different coaching philosophy. Beginning that year, the schedule was increased to 16 games and the pre-season was set at four games. Chicago lost all of its pre-season games but then started the regular season with three straight victories. However, the Bears were only able to finish 7-9, despite winning four of their last five games. It was still a good season for Walter Payton, who gained over a thousand yards for the third-straight season, once again leading the conference. Helping to lead the defense was veteran Alan Page, who had been picked up from the Vikings.

Going into the '79 season, many so called experts had the Bears winning the NFC Central. Mike Phipps started the year at quarterback and led the Bears to an opening day 6-3 win over Green Bay. But Vince Evans took over in the second game, which the Bears lost to Dallas, 24-20. It wasn't Evans's fault though as he threw two touchdowns and ran one in. Chicago regrouped at mid-season and won seven of its last eight to finish at 10-6. The key to that streak was bringing back Mike Phipps as the starting quarterback, who started the comeback with a 28-27 win over the 49ers. Phipps threw a desperation fourth down, 49-yard pass to James Scott for the win. The following week Chicago lost Scott when he broke his ankle and was out for the season. But rookie Rickey Watts was given his chance and had a big day the following week against the Rams, catching six passes against the Rams for 147 yards. The Bears' season came down to their last game against the Cardinals. Chicago and surprising Tampa Bay were tied for first in the Central Division. Chicago needed to beat the Cardinals at home, and Tampa Bay had either to lose or tie. If both Chicago and Tampa Bay won, the Bucs would win the division because of a better divisional record. If that happened, Chicago could still make the playoffs, if the Redskins lost their game with the Cowboys. However, the margin of victory for the Bears' win and a Redskins' loss would have to total at least 33 points. Sound complicated. Nah, not really. The Bears faced an additional distraction on the day of the game. Early on Sunday December 16, George "Mugs" Halas, Jr., the president of the Bears and the son of their founder, died unexpectedly of a heart attack.

The Bears did not let adversity stop them and routed the Cardinals, 42-6. Rickey Watts had a big day, scoring once on an 83-yard kickoff return to open the second half and then once again on a pass reception with time running out. Chicago had won by 36 points and held out some hope. However, Washington had jumped off to a 17-0 lead over Dallas and still led, 34-21, with four minutes left. It didn't look good for the Bears. But then, Washington fumbled, and Dallas scored three plays later. Then Washington was forced to punt, and Roger Staubach threw a touchdown pass to Tony Hill, and Dallas kicked the extra point to win, 35-34! The Bears had made the playoffs!

Chicago traveled to Philadelphia to take on the Eagles. The Bears led, 17-10, at the half, but the Eagles came back to win, 27-17. Walter Payton had an 84-yard run to the Eagles' one-foot line early in the third quarter nullified by a penalty. However, it had been great season for the team and for Payton, who once again rushed for over 1,000 yards for the fourth-straight year. He led the conference with 1,610 yards. Defensively, the Bears finished third in the league, giving up only 249 points and leading in interceptions. It was a good way to end the 1970s and look ahead to the 1980s.

After knocking at the door and making the playoffs in 1977 and 1979, the Bears felt they were back on the road to a title, but Chicago slipped to 7-9 in 1980.

The Bears opened the season with a 12-6 overtime loss to the Packers in Green Bay. The winning touchdown came on a freak play. The Packers' Chester Marcol attempted a field goal which was blocked. However, the ball came back to the surprised Marcol, who ran it in for the winning score. From that auspicious start, the season went straight downhill. The Bears did avenge their opening day loss to the Packers with a 61-7 route at Soldier Field. That equaled a club record for points and established records for first downs and completion percentage.

The next season was a crucial one for coach Neil Armstrong and it proved to be his last in Chicago. The Bears fell to 6-10. It was time for a change after Armstrong was only able to compile a 30-35 record over four seasons.

What about those years?

1. What college did Jim Finks attend?

2. Finks was drafted out of college as a quarterback, but then was converted for a few years to what position?

3. After his playing days were over, Finks took a job as an assistant coach at what college?

4. He then served as general manager of what professional football

team?

5. In what year did Finks lead the NFL in completions and total passing yardage?

6. How many years did Finks spend with the Bears?

7. When did he resign? (date and year)

8. Who took his place?

9. What number did Bob Avellini wear?

10. Where did he go to college?

11. How many years did Avellini play with the Bears?

12. What position did Noah Jackson play?

13. What college did he come from?

14. What number did he wear?

15. How many yards did Roland Harper gain in 1978?

16. How many years was he a Bear?

17. What college was he drafted from?

18. What position did Doug Plank play?

19. Placekicker Bob Thomas went to what college?

20. How long did he play for the Bears?

21. How many life-time points does he have?

22. How many field goals did he make?

23. Where does he rank on the Bears' all-time scoring list?

24. How many field goals of 50 yards or more did he kick?

25. What was his field goal percentage?

26. What was his highest season field goal percentage?

27. What were the most extra points Thomas kicked in a game?

28. In that game how many PAT attempts did he have?

29. In 1975, the Bears moved their pre-season training camp to what location?

30. Who led the 1978 Bears in sacks?

31. How many did he have?

32. How many games did he play?

33. Wide receiver James Scott played how many years with Chicago?

34. What college did he attend?

35. How many passes did he catch in 1977?

36. Who led the Bears in receiving in 1975?

37. How many catches did he have?

38. How many yards did he gain?

39. Where did Dennis Lick attend college?

40. What position did he play?

41. How many years did he play with the Bears?

42. Where did safety Gary Fencik go to college?

43. What number did he wear?

44. Who was the Bears trainer in 1977?

45. Who was his assistant trainer?

46. How many years did Robin Earl play with Chicago?

47. What college did he attend?

48. Neil Armstrong took over as head coach after the 1977 season. What was his position with the Vikings?

49. How long was he at Minnesota?

50. What Bear wore number 50 on the 1977 Bears team?

51. What college did he attend?

52. This running back was picked up by the Bears from the Jets in 1975. Who was he?

53. How many years was he a Bear?

54. What was his number?

55. How many one-point games did the Bears lose in 1976?

56. How many years did Vince Evans play with Chicago?

57. What team did Evans play for in 1994?

58. This Bears great retired after the 1979 season. Who was he?

59. How many years did he play with the Bears?

60. How many games did he play in?

61. Who led the Bears in tackles in 1977 and 1978?

62. How long did Rickey Watts play as a Bear?

63. Who held the snap when Bob Thomas kicked the game winning field goal in sudden death overtime to beat the Giants in 1977?

64. What position did Len Walterscheid play?

65. What college did he attend?

66. How many years did he play with the Bears?

67. Virgil Livers played five positions at what position?

68. What year was he drafted?

69. Who was the Bears public relations director in 1977?

70. Jim Osborne played how many years with the Bears?

71. What position did he play?

72. What college did he attend?

14
The Iron Mike Era: 1982-92

On January 20, 1982, Halas named one of his former players, Mike Ditka, as his new head coach. The former tight end had played for "Papa Bear" from 1961-66, then spent six more seasons with the Cowboys before becoming an assistant coach with them. But he had never lost his love for the Bears and had written Halas a few years prior to 1982, telling him that he would like an opportunity to coach the Bears, if something turned up. Halas remembered that letter and met with Ditka. He offered Ditka a two-year contract, but Iron Mike said he would need three years. Halas said all right, and the deal was struck.

Ditka's first year was during the strike-shortened season of 1982, and the Bears dropped to 3-6. But the Bears once again had started to rebuild. The '82 draft produced quarterback Jim McMahon, Chicago's first pick. They also claimed running back Dennis Gentry.

In 1983, the Bears drafted wide receiver Willie Gault, defensive end Richard Dent, offensive tackle Mark Bortz, and defensive back Dave Duerson. The '83 team climbed to .500. Walter Payton was still going strong, picking up 1,421 yards, averaging 4.5 yards a carry.

In 1984, the Bears improved to 10-6 and won the Central Division to make the playoffs for the first time since 1979. Things were starting to come together. Walter Payton had another big year, rushing for 1,684 yards in his 10th season. The defense was also starting to come together under defensive coordinator Buddy Ryan. With players like Richard Dent, Dan Hampton, Steve McMichael, Mike Singletary, Otis Wilson, and Wilbur Marshall, the Bears' defense was starting to make the rest of the league take notice. Chicago beat the Redskins on the road in the opening game of the playoffs, 23-19, but were shut out the following week by the 49ers, 23-0. But the best was yet to come.

What can you say about the Bears and 1985? Chicago won its first 12 games of the season before being tripped up by the Dolphins, 38-24, in Miami. But Chicago came back and won the final three games of the regular season, then stormed into the playoffs. Chicago shutout the Giants, 21-0, then whitewashed the Rams, 24-0, before totally overpowering the New England Patriots in the Super Bowl, 46-10. The Bears dominating 3-4 defense, which held opponents to just 198 points and an offense, which produced 456 points, were just too much for the rest of the league and resulted in a victory in Super Bowl XIX. The stars were many. Of course, Walter Payton continued to roll, with 1,551 yards rushing and a 4.8 average. The only injustice was that Payton did not score a touchdown in the Super Bowl. One player who did was rookie defensive tackle William Perry, who would go on to become not so famous for his playing ability as for his appetite.

The following year the Bears once again was outstanding, finishing 14-2 during the regular season. But the playoffs were a different story this time. Chicago lost in the first round to the Redskins, 27-13.

In 1987, the Bears were 11-4, good enough for their fourth consecutive Central Division title. But once again, the Redskins ended Chicago's season, with a 21-17 first round playoff win. That game ended the great career of Walter Payton.

In 1988, the Bears once again won the NFC Central with a 12-4 record. By this time, Neil Anderson had taken Walter Payton's job. Chicago advanced to the second round of the playoffs after defeating the Eagles, 20-12, in Chicago. But the following week, Chicago's season ended at the hands of the 49ers, 28-3.

The 1989 season was very erratic. After winning their first four games, the Bears lost to Tampa Bay, Houston, and Cleveland. The Bears did bounce back to beat the Rams, 20-10, but then lost to the Packers, 14-13, in a controversial instant replay call by officials. Chicago did come back the following week with a 20-0 shutout of the Steelers, but that was the last hurrah of the season. Chicago ended up losing its final six games to finish at 6-10. The Bears were out of the playoffs for the first time in five years.

In 1990, Chicago rebounded to 11-5 to win the Central Division. The Bears then won their first round playoff game against the New Orleans Saints, 16-6. But the eventual Super Bowl champs, the New

York Giants, eliminated the Bears in the next game, 31-3. The Bears clearly had to find some answers to compete with the Giants and the 49ers. Incidentally, the loss to the Giants was Dan Hampton's last game.

The 1991 Bears were coach Mike Ditka's last hurrah. In December, he won his 100th regular season game, 27-13, over the Packers at Soldier Field. Chicago finished 11-5 to earn a wild card playoff berth. The Bears were favored in the first round against a rising a Dallas Cowboys team, under third year coach Jimmy Johnson. But the Cowboys upset the Bears, 17-13, at Soldier Field. It was a tough pill to swallow for Ditka and the Bears, and there were calls for Ditka to be replaced.

But Iron Mike was still around when the '92 season began. Physically, there were questions about his health. He had suffered a heart attack, but Ditka was still in control. The Bears were 4-3 after seven games and still very much in the running, but then they lost to the Vikings in game eight, 38-10, at home. The following week Chicago lost once again at home, 31-28, and those losses took the fire out of the Bears. They were only able to win one more game and finished 5-11.

A short time later one of the most successful coaching careers in Bears history ended when Mike Ditka was fired. He had won 106 regular season games, five divisional championships and the Bears only Super Bowl.

What about those years?

1. What Bear led the team in sacks from 1984-87?

2. What college did he attend?

3. Who led the Bears in interceptions in 1988?

4. How long did William Perry play with the Bears?

5. What college did he attend?

6. How long did Steve McMichael play with Chicago?

7. What college did he attend?

8. What team did he play for in 1994?

9. Linebacker Mike Singletary played how many years with the Bears?

10. What college did he go to?

11. How many years did Wilbur Marshall play with Chicago?

12. What college did he attend?

13. How long did Otis Wilson play with Chicago?

14. What college did he attend?

15. How long did Jim McMahon play with the Bear?

16. What were the most touchdown passes he threw in a season as a Bear?

17. In what year did that occur?

18. What was his highest quarterback rating?

19. What year was that?

20. How many times did he throw for 2,000 yards in a season?

21. Who quarterbacked the Bears in 1989?

22. How many times did Neal Anderson gain a thousand yards rushing in a single season?

23. How many rushing touchdowns did he have in 1988?

24. Anderson led the Bears in scoring in 1989. How many points did he have?

25. In what round was tackle Troy Auzenne drafted?

26. When was Mark Carrier drafted?

27. Where does Jim Harbaugh rank on the Bears career passing list?

28. Who leads the Bears in career kickoff returns?

29. How many did he have?

30. What was average per return?

31. How many catches did Emery Moorehead have in his career?

32. What years did he play?

33. How many touchdown catches did he have?

34. How many yards per carry did Brad Muster average?

35. How many punts has Chris Gardocki had blocked?

36. The Bears set a league record in 1981, with how many punts?

37. The '89 Bears defense allowed how many pass completions?

38. The '87 and '88 Bears allowed how many touchdowns each year on the ground?

39. How many seasons did Craig Heyward play with the Bears?

40. Who holds the team record for kickoff returns in a season?

41. How many did he have?

42. Who holds the team record for consecutive completions?

43. How many did he have?

44. What quarterback holds the single season completion percentage mark?

45. Who has played in the most Bears' post-season games?

46. How many has he played in?

47. Two Bears have called for fair catches on five punts in a single game. Name them.

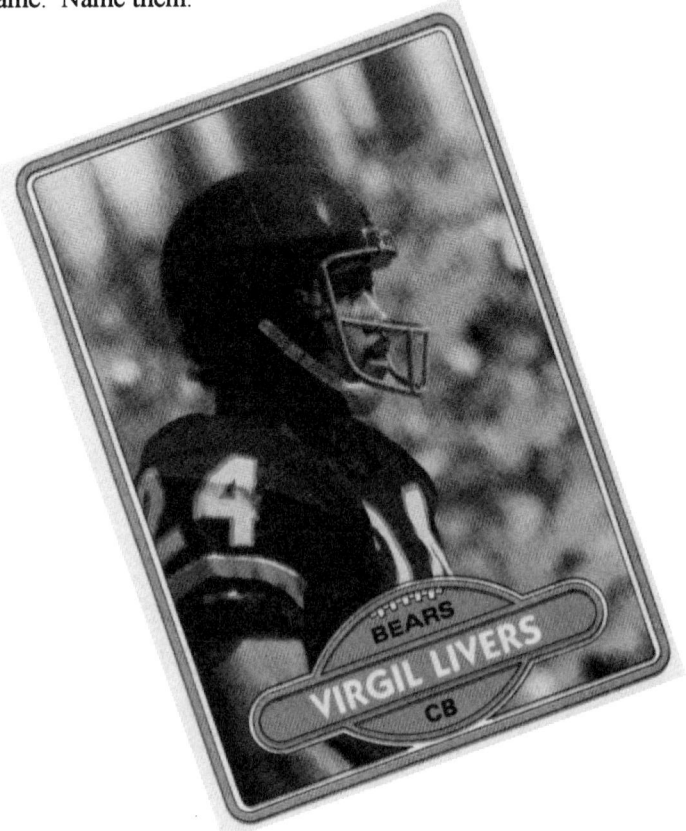

15
Rebuilding Again: 1993-Present

On January 19, 1993, Dave Wannstedt was named the new head coach of the Chicago Bears. He had served for four years as defensive coordinator of the Dallas Cowboys and was sought after by a number of teams. Wannstedt became the 11th Bears' coach in team history.

The '93 Bears finished 7-9. After an 0-2 start, Chicago won three-straight games. Later in the season, the Bears put together a four-game winning streak, including a league first, three road wins in 12 days. Chicago was in a first place tie with four games remaining in the regular season, when the season suddenly came to an end with a four game losing streak. But once again, the Bears and their new head coach were hoping to fight their way back to the top.

In 1994, the 75th anniversary of the NFL, the Bears began with a 21-9 win over Tampa Bay at Soldier Field. It was their 35th season opening win, the most in league history. Chicago then lost two in a row and also lost their starting quarterback Eric Kramer, with an injured shoulder. But then Steve Walsh stepped in for Kramer and led the Bears to three straight wins. After two straight losses, the Bears put together a four game winning streak. Chicago finished at 9-7 and went on the road to play the central division champs, the Minnesota Vikings. Chicago dominated 35-18 and advanced to the second round against the San Francisco 49ers. The 49ers defeated the Bears, 44-15, and went on to win their fifth Super Bowl. Despite the loss, the Bears had made it back to the playoffs and that was a triumph in itself.

Going into 1995, the Bears hope to improve on their fourth place finish in the NFC central. The '94 offense was ranked 23rd overall, which was a big improvement from the year before. It appears as if Chicago may have found the quarterback they've been looking for in Steve Walsh. As for receivers, the Bears have a good corps in Jeff Graham, who caught the most passes by a Bear in 25 years, along with Curtis Conway. On the ground, Lewis Tillman gained 899 yards and scored seven touchdowns. The offensive line allowed only 25 sacks in '94, the eighth best in the league. Defensively, it was a bend but don't break unit. The Bears were the toughest team in the conference to score against inside the 20 and allowed only four scoring plays longer than 20 yards. Veteran Trace Armstrong led the team in sacks with 7.5, while Alonzo Spellman had seven in his first season playing full time.

In the April '95 draft, Chicago's first pick was Colorado star running back, Rashaan Salaam. Considering the success of such former Bears' running backs like Red Grange, Willie Galimore, Gale Sayers, Walter Payton, and Neal Anderson, to name a few, Chicago could soon have another star in its backfield.

So the future at this point appears bright for Dave Wannstedt and the Bears. Probably somewhere, the Papa Bear himself is nodding his head in approval.

What about those years?

1. How many years did Dave Wannstedt coach as an assistant at Oklahoma State?

2. How long did he coach with the Dallas Cowboys?

3. Where did he play college football?

4. What team selected him in the draft?

5. What team did he beat for his first NFL coaching victory?

6. What was the score?

7. How many times has Kevin Butler scored more than 100 points in a season?

Chicago Bears Facts & Trivia

8. What was his highest point total in a season?

9. In what year?

10. How many consecutive games have the Bears won when rushing for at least forty times in a game?

11. Lewis Tillman had the Bears' longest run from scrimmage in the '94 regular season. How long was it?

12. Raymont Harris had the Bears' longest run in the '94 playoffs. How long was it?

13. What is the Bears record against the Green Bay Packers?

14. What is the Bears record against the Cardinals?

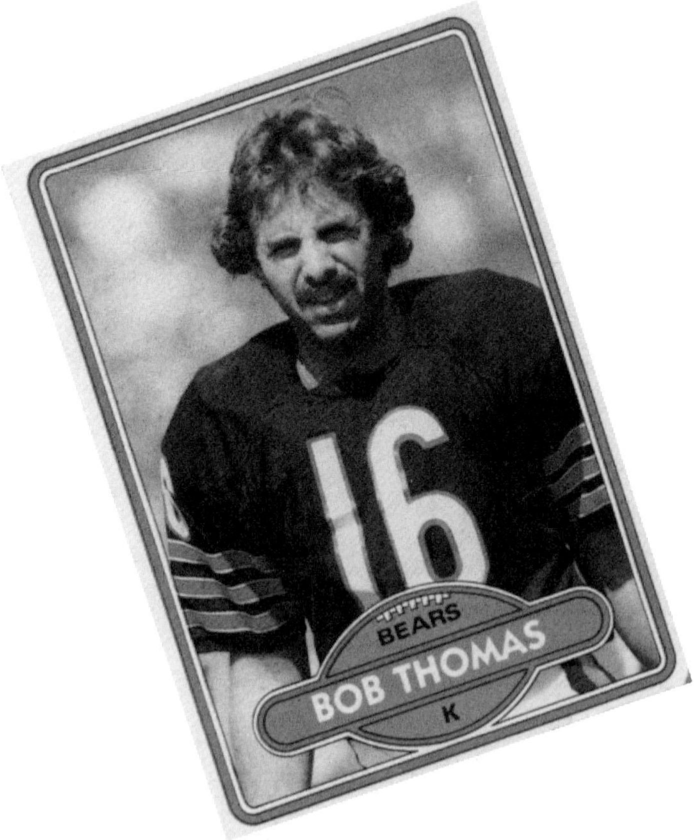

16
BEARS
BOB THOMAS
K

A Few Good Bears

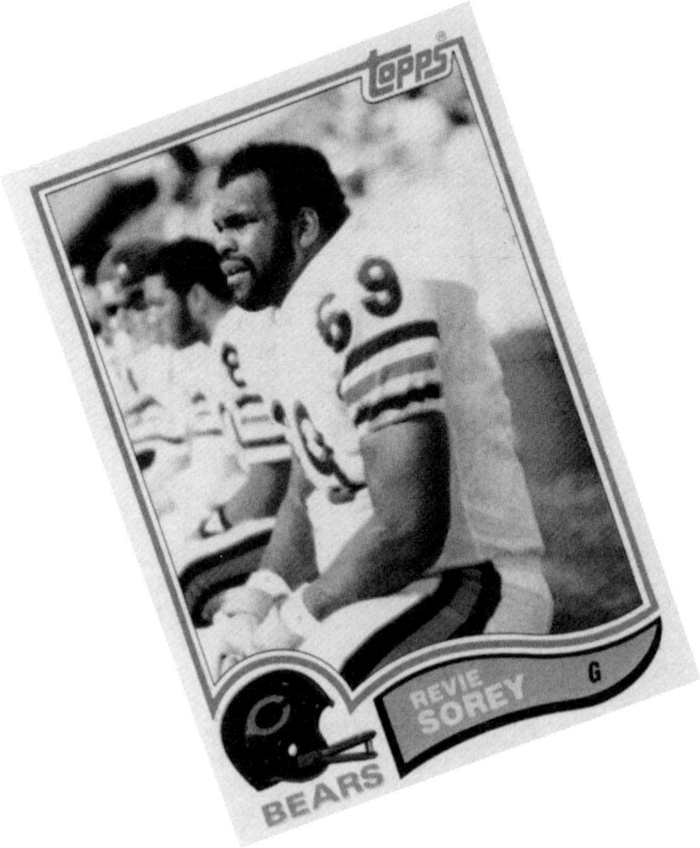
topps
69
REVIE
SOREY
G
BEARS

1
Mike Ditka

The intense Ditka thoroughly defined what a tight end should be. He not only had size and strength to block, but he also was a top receiver who could run with the football once he caught it. That meant running over the opposition more times than running around them.

Ditka was the consummate pro who directed his fury on the field to beating the opposing team. His talent and drive made him a perennial pro bowler.

After six seasons with the Bears, he spent six more with the Dallas Cowboys before becoming one of their assistant coaches. But his love for the Bears and his respect for George Halas led to his being hired by "Papa Bear" in 1982 as the Bears' head coach. He rebuilt the team and led the Bears to their only Super Bowl win.

Mike Ditka was an ideal tight end who, with a combination of talent, hard work, and a burning desire to win, not only was successful on the field but on the sidelines as well as a coach.

What about Mike Ditka?

1. As a player, Mike Ditka holds the distinction of being what?

2. Ditka set a team rookie reception record in 1961. How many passes did he catch?

3. How many times was he selected to the Pro Bowl as a Bear?

4. Ditka was drafted in 1961 out of Pittsburgh. What round was he taken in?

5. How many times did Ditka coach the Bears to the NFC championship game?

6. How many times did he lead the Bears in receiving and scoring?

7. What number did Ditka wear with the Bears?

2
Dick Butkus

While some players display skill and others ferocity, Butkus had both —in abundance. He not only had the desire but the talent to become, arguably, the best middle linebacker ever to play the game. Week in and week out, the snarling Butkus dominated offensive linemen, terrorized quarterbacks, and punished anyone with the ball. Anyone ever hit by Butkus did not relish the thought of going through that experience again.

During his career, Butkus brought the middle linebacker position to new heights, and he became the model for future generations of linebackers. When you think of the Bears' defense of the mid-1960s to the early 1970s, one name stands out: Dick Butkus.

What about Dick Butkus?

1. How many years did Butkus play with the Bears?

2. How many fumble recoveries did he have?

3. Where does he rank in the history of the league in that category?

4. He led the Bears in interceptions in 1965 with how many?

5. How many take-aways did he have in 1965?

6. What overall pick was Butkus in the 1965 draft?

7. In what year was he voted to his first Pro Bowl?

8. How many times was he voted to the Pro Bowl?

9. What college did he attend?

10. In what year was he inducted into the Pro Football Hall of Fame?

11. What professions did he take up after his playing career came to an end?

3
Gale Sayers

"The Kansas Comet" took football by storm in his rookie season of 1965. His electrifying runs dazzled teammates, coaches, opposing teams, and, of course, the fans. His running was pure poetry in motion, and no other running back before him was able to change direction so suddenly on a football field. Every time Sayers touched the football, the other team knew he had the potential of scoring, and it seemed as though those first few seasons he did. As Sayers went, so went the Bears.

However, his greatness was short-lived, and after two serious knee injuries, he was forced to retire. Sayers's election to the Pro Football Hall of Fame was just a formality. Although his stay in the NFL was short, Gale Sayers's gifted running and style will never be forgotten.

What about Gale Sayers?

1. Gale Sayers won the Rookie of the Year award in 1965. Who came in second in the voting?

2. How many years did he lead the league in rushing and when were those years?

3. How many 100-yard rushing games did he have in his career?

4. How many yards per carry did he average?

5. What university did Sayers attend?

6. What pick overall in the first round was he?

7. Of Sayers's six touchdowns in one game in 1965, four were on the ground. How long were they?

8. How long was the screen pass he caught for a touchdown?

9. How long was the punt return he had for a touchdown?

10. Two other players had scored six touchdowns in the a game before Sayers and ironically both came against the Bears. Who scored the touchdowns and for what teams?

11. Sayers led the Bears in rushing in 1965 with how many yards?

12. What number did Sayers wear?

13. How many yards did Sayers gain in his career and where does he rank on the all time Bears rushing list?

14. How many times did Sayers rush for 200 yards in a game?

15. What was his signing bonus?

4
"The Gallopin' Ghost"

The second superstar of professional football, after Jim Thorpe, joined the Bears on Thanksgiving Day, 1925.

Only five days after his final game at the University of Illinois against Ohio State, Harold "Red" Grange donned a Chicago Bears uniform and took the field against the Chicago Cardinals. On a muddy field, Grange managed to only gain 36 yards on 16 carries. He was also 0-6 in the passing department. Needless to say, the game ended in a scoreless tie. Just three days later, 28,000 fans braved a snowstorm to see Grange rush for 72 yards, return a kickoff for 28 more yards, and catch two passes as the Bears beat the Columbus Tigers, 14-13.

The first tour of Grange and the Bears started with them playing eight games in 12 days in eight different cities. After a 10-day rest, they played eight more games over the course of a month. The Bears wound up traveling by train from Chicago to Florida, west to California, and north to Seattle. Grange earned an estimated $200,000 from the tour, and he was selected to his first All-Professional Team, along with team-mates Ed Healey and Joe Sternaman.

The highlight came when over 75,000 fans turned out to see Red and the Bears defeat a make-up team called the LA Tigers, 17-7. The Red Grange tour was a giant step toward popularizing the game of football.

What about Red Grange?

1. What was Grange's hometown?

2. What number did Grange wear as a Bear?

3. How many years did Grange play with the Bears?

4. Grange left the Bears in 1926 to play for what team?

5. Against what team did Grange suffer a serious knee injury?

6. Besides running back, what other position did Grange play?

7. In what year was he named to the all-NFL team?

8. Name Grange's first business manager.

9. Besides "The Gallopin' Ghost", what other nickname did he have?

10. What was the nickname of Grange's second business manager?

11. Name five items that carried Red's name or that he endorsed in 1925.

12. After meeting Grange for the first time, this man reportedly said, "Young man, I always liked animal acts ." Who was he?

13. What was the record of the 1925 Bears during the regular season?

Bear Tracks

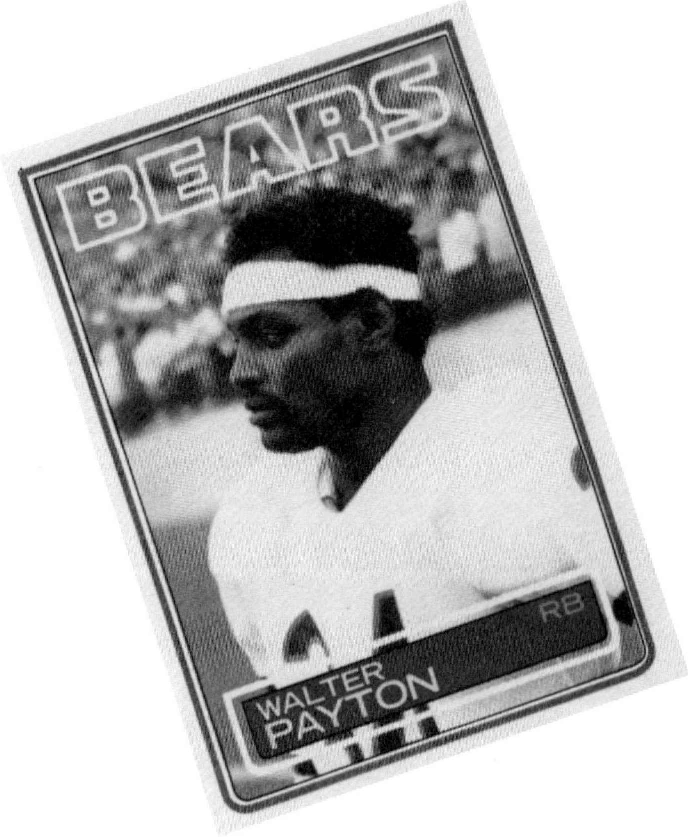
BEARS
RB
WALTER
PAYTON

I
Chronology

1920
September 17 - George Halas, representing A.E. Staley, meets with representatives of 12 other clubs in Ralph Hay's Hupmobile showroom in Canton, Ohio. Staley receives a franchise for his company football team, popularly known as the Decatur Staleys, to play in newly formed American Professional Football Association, later reorganized and renamed the National Football League.
November 28 - Staleys play Chicago Cardinals for first time, losing, 7-6. Cardinals, who move to St. Louis in 1960, then Arizona in 1988, are only original NFL franchise to remain in operation continuously since league's inception.

1921
October - Decatur Staleys become Chicago Staleys and contract to play all home games at Cubs Park, later known as Wrigley Field. A.E. Staley gives George Halas and his partner Ed "Dutch" Sternaman the team and $5,000 to keep the Staleys name for that season. The Staleys go 9-1-1 to win the APFA title.

1922
January 27 - Refusing to become embroiled in a dispute between Halas and Bill Harley, who claims to be in partnership with Halas and Sternaman, A.E. Staley surrenders his franchise in APFA. Halas requests franchise in APFA for Chicago. Harley claims Staley franchise and also makes request to put team in Chicago.
January 28 - To settle the dispute between Harley and Halas,

league officials vote to give each man a franchise in the APFA. Harley receives right to field a team in Toledo, while Halas is granted a franchise for Chicago which he officially names the Chicago Bears.

November 27 - Bears make their first player deal, purchasing tackle Ed Healey's contract from Rock Island Independents for $100.

1923

October 14 - Bears-Packers rivalry begins with Bears beating Packers in Green Bay, 3-0.

1925

November 22 - With the completion of his college career, Harold "Red" Grange signs to play with the Bears.

November 26 - Bears begin a 16-game coast-to-coast tour on Thanksgiving Day in Chicago ending two months later. Bears record for the tour was ll-4-l. 36,000 fans pay to see Grange's first game. "The Gallopin' Ghost" is held to 36 yards as Bears and Cardinals play to a scoreless tie.

December 6 - Bears play New Giants for first time and win at Polo Grounds in New York, 19-7.

1926

January 26 - Bears beat all-star team named the Los Angeles Tigers in LA Coliseum, 17-7, in front of 75,000 fans. Grange scores two touchdowns.

1930

Halas and Sternaman agree to replace themselves as head coaches with Ralph Jones. Jones coaches three seasons and posts a record of 24-10-7.

October 22 - Bears play Portsmouth Spartans for the first time. Spartans move to Detroit and renamed Lions in 1934.

December 15 - Football's first indoor game is played on an 80-yard field inside Chicago Stadium. Bears beat Cardinals in an exhibition game, 9-7, before 10,000 fans.

1932

October 30 - Bears play Boston Braves for first time. Braves

Chicago Bears Facts & Trivia

renamed Redskins next year, then move to Washington in 1937.
December 18 - Bears beat Portsmouth Spartans 9-0, for the NFL Championship. The game is played inside Chicago Stadium on an 80-yard field.
Sternaman sells his half of the club to Halas after the franchise loses $18,000.

1933
Halas returns to coach the Bears.
November 5 - Bears' 16-game unbeaten streak stopped with loss to Boston Redskins.
November 12 - Bears play Philadelphia Eagles for first time.
December 17 - Bears defeat New York Giants, 23-21 in the NFL's first championship game.

1934
Halas University, which is the Bears Alumni Association, is begun.
August 31 - Champion Bears and the first College All-Star team play to a scoreless tie at Soldier Field. The game was sponsored by the Chicago Tribune Charities.
October 10 - Bears play Pittsburgh Pirates for first time. Pirates renamed Steelers in 1937.
December 2 - Bears' rookie Beattie Feathers becomes first pro football player to rush for 1,000 yards. He finishes with 1,004 to lead league.
December 9 - Undefeated Bears lose to Giants in the title game at the Polo Grounds, 30-13. Bears led, 10-3, at the half.

1936
Joe Stydahar, West Virginia tackle, is club's first ever draft pick.

1937
October 10 - Bears play Cleveland Rams first time ever. Rams move to Los Angeles 1946, then move to St. Louis 1995.
December 12 - After winning Western Division, Bears lose NFL championship game to Redskins at Wrigley Field, 28-21.

1940
December 8 - Bears post biggest championship win ever, routing Redskins, 73-0, in Washington. 10 different Bears score TDs.

1942
December 13 - Bears lose title game to Redskins at Washington, 14-6. Prior to game, Halas leaves for U. S. Navy. For the next three years while Halas is in the service, Bears are coached by Hunk Anderson and Luke Johnsos, who compile a 15-11-2 record.

1943
November 14 - Sid Luckman passes for 433 yards and seven touchdowns against Giants to become the first quarterback to pass for over 400 yards in a game.

December 26 - Bears win another title, beating Redskins at Wrigley Field, 41-21. Over 34,000 fans see Luckman throw five TD passes. Also, Bronko Nagurski scores his last touchdown, a three-yard run.

1946
December 15 - With Halas back as coach, Bears beat Giants before an NFL record title game crowd of over 58,000 at the Polo Grounds, 24-14.

1948
Bears make the first trade for a draft choice, then select quarterback Bobby Layne.

1949
December 11 - Johnny Lujack sets a league passing record, throwing for 468 yards against Cardinals.

1950
September 24 - Bears play San Francisco 49ers for first time.

December 17 - Bears and Rams tie for Western Division title, but Rams win playoff game in LA, 24-14.

1951
November 25 - Bears play Cleveland Browns first time ever.

1953
September 27 - Bears play Baltimore Colts first time ever. Colts move to Indianapolis in 1984.

1956
Halas retires as head coach, and Paddy Driscoll is hired.
December 30 - Bears lose NFL title game to Giants at Yankee Stadium, 47-7.

1958
Halas returns as head coach. Driscoll is named vice-president and demoted to assistant coach.
November 2 - A league attendance record is set as Bears and Rams draw 90,833 fans at the LA Coliseum. Bears lose, 41-35.

1960
November 27 - Bears play Dallas Cowboys first time ever.

1961
September 17 - Bears play Minnesota Vikings first time ever.

1963
December 29 - Bears defeat Giants in NFL title game at Wrigley Field, 14-10. Bears intercept Y.A. Tittle five times. Quarterback Bill Wade scores both Bear touchdowns on two- and one-yard runs.

1964
Johnny Morris sets league record by catching 93 passes.

1965
Bears draft linebacker Dick Butkus and running back Gale Sayers in first round.
December 12 - Sayers scores six touchdowns against 49ers. Sayers scores 22 touchdowns on the season.

1966
November 27 - Bears play Atlanta Falcons first time ever.
Sayers sets a league combined yardage record of 2,440 yards.

1968
May 27 - George Halas retires as coach for the final time after 40 years at the helm. The all-time winningest coach at that time, Halas finished with 324 wins, 151 defeats, and 31 ties. Jim Dooley takes over as coach.
December 1 - Bears play New Orleans Saints first time ever.

1970
Halas elected president of the National Football Conference as NFL and AFL merge.
June 16 - Running back Brian Piccolo dies of cancer. The Piccolo fund is established by the club for cancer research.
October 18 - Bears play San Diego Chargers first time ever.
November 22 - Bears play Buffalo Bills first time ever.
December 13 - Bears play their last game at Wrigley Field, beating the Packers, 35-17.

1971
September 19 - Bears open the season at their new home at Soldier Field, by defeating the Steelers, 17-15.
November 29 - Bears play Miami Dolphins first time ever.
December 5 - Bears play Denver Broncos first time ever.

1972
November 26 - Bears play Cincinnati Bengals first time ever.
December 17 - Bears play Oakland Raiders first time ever. Raiders move to Los Angeles 1982.

1973
October 28 - Bears play Houston Oilers first time ever.
November 12 - Bears play Kansas City Chiefs first time ever.

1974
September 12 - Jim Finks becomes vice president and general manager.

September 15 - Bears play New York Jets first time ever.
December 17 - Abe Gibron leaves as head coach after three seasons and a record of 11-30-1.
December 31 - Jack Pardee, a former NFL star linebacker, takes over as coach and becomes the first non-Bear to hold that position.

1975
Walter Payton joins Bears and would play through 1987.

1976
December 5 - Bears play Seattle Seahawks first time ever.

1977
November 20 - Payton rushes for league record 275 yards against Vikings at Soldier Field. That season, Payton would rush for a Bear record 1,852 yards.
December 4 - Bears play Tampa Bay Buccaneers first time ever.
December 18 - Bears go 9-5, clinch their first playoff spot in 14 years with a 12-9 overtime win over the Giants.
December 26 - Bears lose, 37-7, in the playoffs to Dallas.

1978
January 19 - Jack Pardee resigns as coach after a three-year record of 20-22.
February 16 - Neil Armstrong is named the new head coach. Armstrong had been the Vikings defensive coordinator.

1979
December 16 - George "Mugs" Halas, Jr., the son of the Bears founder, dies suddenly of a massive heart attack. Chicago wins that day, 42-6, over St. Louis, while Dallas edges Washington, 35-34, to put Bears into the playoffs.
December 23 - Bears lose the wild card playoff game to the Eagles at Philadelphia, 27-17.

1980
October 6 - Walter Payton raises his lifetime combined yardage mark to 9,492, as he moves past Gale Sayers's old record, in a 23-0 win over Tampa Bay.

December 7 - Bears trounce the Packers, 61-7, at Soldier Field.

1982
January 4 - Neil Armstrong leaves as head coach after a four-year record of 30-35.
January 20 - Former Bears' tight end Mike Ditka, who had also been a player and an assistant coach with Dallas, becomes the new head coach.

1983
August 24 - Finks resigns after nine seasons as general manager.
October 5 - Jerry Vainisi is named by George Halas as the new general manager.
October 31 - George Halas dies at the age of 88.
November 11 - Michael McCaskey becomes the third team president in Bears' history.

1984
October 7 - Walter Payton rushes for 154 yards against Saints to move past Jim Brown as the league's all-time leading rusher. The record came on a six-yard run in the third quarter.
November 25 - Bears clinch their first Central Division title with a 34-3 route of the Vikings at Minneapolis.
December 30 - Bears win over Redskins 23-19 in divisional playoffs but lose in the NFC championship game to 49ers, 23-0.

1985
After winning first 12 games, the Bears post 15-1 regular season mark en route to second straight divisional title. Nine Bears are selected for the Pro Bowl.

1986
January 5 - Bears host first playoff game since 1963 championship season and shutout the Giants, 21-0.
January 12 - Bears advance to their first Super Bowl after shutting out Rams, 24-0, in the NFC title game at Soldier Field.
January 26 - Bears rout the New England Patriots, 46-10, in Super Bowl XX and in the process set seven Super Bowl records.

The following day an estimated 500,000 people turn out to greet the team in a ticker tape parade in downtown Chicago.
Bears finish 14-2 and win third straight Central Division title. The defense allows a record low 187 points. However, Chicago is eliminated in the opening round of playoffs by Washington, 27-13.

1987
December 20 - Walter Payton plays his final regular season game at Soldier Field. Prior to the game, his jersey number 34 is retired.

In a strike interrupted season, the Bears finish 11-4 and win their fourth consecutive Central Division crown. Chicago loses in the playoffs to Redskins, 21-17.

1988
Bears finish 12-4 during the regular season, which tied for the best record in the league. Chicago then advance to the NFC title game but lose to 49ers. From 1984 through 1988, Bears won 62 games, most ever by a team over a five-year span.

1989
Kevin Butler sets a league record with his 24th consecutive field goal.

December 24 - Richard Dent becomes Bears' all-time sack leader, surpassing Jim Osborne.

1990
Two Chicago businessmen, Andy McKenna and Patrick G. Ryan, purchase about twenty percent of the team from the McCaskeys.

Bears go 11-5, win Central Division title, then go on to first round playoff victory over Saints, 16-6, before losing to Giants, 31-3, in Dan Hampton's final game.

1991
December 8 - Bears beat Packers at Lambeau Field, Green Bay, 27-13, for Mike Ditka's 100th regular season victory.

Chicago earns a wild card playoff berth after an 11-5 season, but in the playoffs, Dallas upsets Bears at Soldier Field, 17-13.

1992

October 4 - Kevin Butler passes Walter Payton as the Bears all-time leading scorer. Payton had scored 750 points but was passed when Butler hit a 50 yard field goal.

December 13 - 10-time Pro Bowler Mike Singletary plays his final home game as Bears upset the Steelers, 30-6.

1993

Mike Ditka is fired as coach. He coached the team to six NFC Central Division titles and the Bears' only Super Bowl victory.

January 19 - Dave Wannstedt is named to replace Ditka. Wannstedt is the 11th coach in Bears history.

October 3 - Bears reach another milestone, playing their 1,000th game, defeating Falcons at Soldier Field, 6-0.

Bears finish 7-9 in Wannstedt's first season.

1994

Bears make playoffs as Wild Card entry with 9-7 record.

1995

January 1 - Bears beat Vikings in Minneapolis in first round of playoffs, 35-18, before losing in the second round to the eventual Super Bowl champs, the San Francisco 49ers.

Bears announce that a new stadium will be built and that they will leave Soldier Field by 1999.

2
The Bears vs. The NFL

The Chicago Bears were not born until George Halas was granted a franchise by the league on January 28, 1922. The NFL considers the Decatur Staleys and the Chicago Staleys to have been the Bears by another name. This is the same method of re-writing history that Major League Baseball uses when it claims the Abner Doubleday invented baseball in 1839. Many arguments could be made to support the NFL's stand, and just as many could be made to support the juxtaposition that the Staleys were one franchise and the Bears were and are a separate franchise. For now, we'll go along with the NFL.

Regular Season Record

OPPONENT	W	L	T
Akron Indians	1	0	0
Akron Pros	2	0	1
Arizona Cardinals	**1**	**0**	**0**
Atlanta Falcons	**9**	**9**	**0**
Baltimore Colts	13	21	0
Boston Braves-Redskins	4	1	1
Boston Yanks	3	0	0
Brooklyn Dodgers	6	0	1
Buffalo All-Americans	3	1	0
Buffalo Bills	**4**	**2**	**0**
Buffalo Bison	1	1	0
Canton Bulldogs	2	2	0
Card-Pitt	2	0	0
Chicago Cardinals	45	19	6
Chicago Tigers	2	0	0
Cincinnati Bengals	**2**	**3**	**0**
Cincinnati Reds	2	0	0
Cleveland Browns	**3**	**6**	**0**

Cleveland Bulldogs	2	1	0
Cleveland Indians	1	0	0
Cleveland Rams	11	5	0
Cleveland Tigers	1	0	0
Columbus Tigers	2	0	0
Dallas Cowboys	6	8	0
Dallas Texans	1	1	0
Dayton Triangles	4	0	0
Denver Broncos	**5**	**5**	**0**
Detroit Lions	**70**	**48**	**3**
Detroit Panthers	3	1	1
Detroit Wolverines	0	2	0
Duluth Eskimos	2	0	0
Frankford Yellow Jackets	7	4	2
Green Bay Packers	**81**	**61**	**6**
Hammond Pros	3	0	0
Houston Oilers	**2**	**4**	**0**
Indianapolis Colts	**3**	**0**	**0**
Kansas City Chiefs	**4**	**2**	**0**
Los Angeles Raiders	2	2	0
Los Angeles Rams	34	24	3
Louisville Colonels	1	0	0
Miami Dolphins	**2**	**5**	**0**
Milwaukee Badgers	3	0	1
Minneapolis Redjackets	5	0	0
Minnesota Vikings	**29**	**36**	**2**
New England Patriots	**2**	**4**	**0**
New Orleans Saints	**9**	**6**	**0**
New York Giants	**24**	**16**	**2**
New York Jets	**4**	**1**	**0**
New York Yankees	5	2	0
Oakland Raiders	**1**	**3**	**0**
Oorang Indians	2	0	0
Philadelphia Eagles	**24**	**4**	**1**
Phoenix Cardinals	1	0	0
Pittsburgh Pirates-Steelers	**16**	**4**	**1**
Portsmouth Spartans	4	2	2
Pottsville Maroons	3	0	0
Providence Steam Roller	0	1	1
Racine Legion	2	0	2
Rochester Jeffersons	2	0	0
Rock Island Independents	8	1	4
St. Louis Cardinals	5	6	0
San Diego Chargers	**2**	**4**	**0**
San Francisco 49ers	**25**	**25**	**1**
Seattle Seahawks	**2**	**4**	**0**
Staten Island Stapletons	1	0	1
Tampa Bay Buccaneers	**26**	**8**	**0**
Toledo Maroons	1	0	0
Washington Redskins	**14**	**11**	**0**

Bear Answers

1 - In the Beginning: 1920-24
1. February 2, 1895
2. Frank and Barbara
3. University of Illinois
4. New York Yankees, right field, Babe Ruth
5. End
6. Hunk
7. 164
8. 21
9. Tackle
10. Milliken
11. Guard
12. Tackle
13. Blackwood Hotel
14. The "T-Formation"
15. Jim Thorpe
16. End
17. 10 years (1920-29)
18. 1933
19. Six
20. 324
21. #7
22. 1968
23. Bill Harley
24. 15 % of the gross gate plus all the concessions. When the gross receipts reached $10,000, the rental would increase to 20 %.
25. The Staleys
26. 20-0
27. Chicago
28. Pard Pearce, Pete Stinchcomb & George Halas
29. Fullback
30. One

2 - The Second Crown: 1925-32
1. Boxing
2. Luke Johnsos
3. 24
4. University of Minnesota
5. Clarence Spears
6. Five
7. Joe Savoldi
8. Notre Dame
9. Fullback
10. Three
11. One
12. Halfback
13. Monmouth (Illinois) College
14. Seven
15. Red Grange
16. 37 points
17. Six
18. Gardie Grange
19. Three years
20. End
21. Green Bay
22. 2-0
23. Three
24. None
25. Tackle

3 - Halas Returns to the Helm: 1933-34
1. U. of Minnesota
2. Automatic Jack
3. 76
4. 14
5. 72 consecutive PAT's
6. 10
7. Lou Groza, 13, 1950
8. U. of Tennessee
9. 9.94
10. 5.8
11. Four years
12. 15th
13. 14
14. 5-1-1
15. Arch Ward
16. Seven
17. 1947
18. 16-0
19. Three
20. He could throw a pass behind his back.
21. John
22. Six
23. A helmet
24. Bronko Nagurski
25. Gene Ronzani
26. $210.34
27. Two, against the Boston Redskins and the Brooklyn Dodgers
28. Steve Owen
29. Manhattan College basketball team

30. New York Giants
31. 10-9
32. Carl Brumbaugh
33. Florida
34. 1930
35. Eight
36. Bob Elson

4 - Up and Down: 1935-39
1. Don Hutson
2. Gerald Ford
3. Irv Kupcinet
4. Joe Kopcha, George Musso and Bill Karr
5. Kopcha (guard), Musso (tackle), Karr (end)
6. Joe Stydahar
7. U. of West Virginia
8. Danny Fortman
9. Guard
10. Colgate
11. Eggs
12. Philadelphia Eagles
13. Les McDonald
14. End
15. U. of Nebraska
16. Philadelphia Eagles
17. Sam Francis
18. Fullback
19. 42-28
20. The last four minutes were not played because of darkness.
21. On a 10-yard run
22. On a 37-yard touchdown pass
23. Pro Wrestling
24. The Pro Bowl
25. Bill Osmanski
26. 699

5 - Sweet Revenge and Defeat: 1940-42
1. 10 different players
2. Fullback Bill Osmanski
3. Harry Clark
4. 15
5. One
6. Three
7. Two
8. Bob Snyder
9. Because the officials only had one football left.
10. Duke
11. Bulldog
12. Hardin-Simmons

13. Texas
14. 13 seasons and six times an all pro
15. Linebacker
16. Joe Osmanski
17. Fullback
18. 48 completions for 941 yards
19. Danny Fortmann and Joe Stydahar
20. Chicago Cardinals and Detroit Lions
21. 37-13
22. Tom Harmon
23. 36
24. 14 points
25. 53
26. Chicago Cardinals
27. Andy Lotshaw
28. Ralph Brizzolara
29. Scooter McLean
30. 54
31. Young Bussey
32. Hampton Pool
33. Detroit Lions
34. Bulldog Turner
35. Eight
36. Gary Famiglietti
37. 503
38. Lee Artoe
39. Tackle
40. Hugh Gallarneau

6 - Hunk, Luke, and Paddy, But No Papa Bear: 1943-45
1. He threw 7 touchdowns and passed for 433 yards
2. 28
3. Two, 194
4. Harry Clark 2; Dante Magnani 2; and Jim Benton 1.
5. He served as a welfare and recreation officer
6. Admiral Chester Nimitz
7. $1,146, the most ever paid up to that time
8. St. Joseph's College in Rensselaer, Indiana
9. 31
10. Ed Sprinkle
11. 12
12. Hardin Simmons
13. Bulldog Turner
14. Bob Steuber
15. Ninth
16. Missouri
17. Al Hoptowit
18. Dom Sigillo

Chicago Bears Facts & Trivia

19. Packers, Steelers and Cardinals
20. In each win, the Bears scored 28 points
21. George McAfee

7 - Climbing Back: 1946-50
1. 17
2. Dante Magnani
3. 39 yards
4. Jim Keane
5. 64
6. 910
7. 10
8. 13
9. 44
10. Three
11. Sid Luckman, Ken Kavanaugh and Fred Davis
12. One year at Holy Cross and two years at Notre Dame
13. Eight
14. Five times
15. 1975
16. Connor was selected a Pro Bowler in 1951 and 1952 on both offense and defense
17. Eight
18. Two
19. Los Angeles Rams
20. LA Coliseum
21. The Bears Quarterback Club
22. W-E-N-R
23. Channel 7
24. U. of Kentucky
25. 541
26. 88
27. Five
28. 83
29. Kevin Butler (80. through the end of the '94 season and Bob Thomas, 55.
30. Two
31. 1948
32. Texas
33. 14
34. 193
35. 6'4" - 215 lbs
36. Curly
37. Fullback
38. Four
39. Dick Barwegan
40. Purdue
41. Three seasons
42. Rykovich
43. Halfback

44. U. of Illinois
45. #32
46. Al Campana
47. On a run
48. 23
49. George Gulyanics
50. 571
51. Seven
52. Johnny Lujack, George Connor, Dick Barwegan, Bulldog Turner, Ed Sprinkle, Fred Davis, and Ray Bray

8 - Struggling: 1951-57
1. John
2. 670
3. U. of Mississippi
4. One
5. Chicago Cardinals
6. Boris
7. Halfback
8. Nine
9. College of the Pacific
10. Halfback
11. 30
12. 6.5
13. Two
14. Curly Morrison
15. 367 yards
16. Florence State Teachers College
17. Alabama
18. Eight
19. 19
20. Three
21. 214 yards
22. 10/31/54
23. Two
24. Seven
25. 1954
26. 4,616
27. 40
28. U. of Illinois
29. 10
30. Running back
31. Two
32. Rick Casares
33. 2,468 (led league)
34. 22 (led league.)
35. 140 (led league)
36. Five
37. Rick Casares, Bill George, Stan Jones, Larry Strickland and Harlon Hill
38. Jim Dooley
39. 37
40. 530

41. Johnny Unitas
42. Los Angeles Rams
43. Willie Galimore
44. Florida A & M
45. Seven
46. 37
47. 2,985
48. 26
49. Third
50. $6,500-$14,200

9 - Papa Bear Returns Again: 1958-62
1. Los Angeles Rams
2. Ends coach
3. Eight seasons
4. Los Angeles Rams
5. Santa Barbara
6. 10 years
7. Returned punts and kickoffs
8. 356
9. 30
10. 1,200 yards
11. 1964
12. 15
13. Six
14. 1964
15. 201 yards
16. 50 yard dash
17. 5.2 seconds
18. Television Sports Announcer
19. Washington Redskins
20. No relation
21. Georgia Tech
22. Seven
23. Ed Brown, Zeke Bratkowski and Rudy Bukich
24. Two
25. Guard
26. Purdue
27. Seven
28. Three
29. 11-30-1
30. 1972-74
31. Green Bay Packers
32. Grambling
33. Indiana
34. Mike Pyle
35. Nine
36. 84 yards
37. Six seasons
38. 56 %
39. Three times
40. Bo Farrington
41. Four seasons

42. Detroit Lions
43. Linebacker
44. Seven
45. Seven
46. 51.4%
47. Ronnie Bull
48. Baylor
49. Nine
50. #67

10 - Champions: 1963
1. 10.1
2. 103 per game
3. Seven
4. 36
5. Rosey Taylor
6. Nine
7. $5,879
8. 17-17 & 17-17
9. George Allen
10. Six
11. Mike Ditka, Richie Petitbon, Rosey Taylor, Doug Atkins, Bill George and Joe Fortunato
12. Ed Rozy
13. Three
14. George Halas, Red Grange and Bronko Nagurski
15. Two and one yard runs
16. Billy Martin
17. The 30th anniversary of the first world championship game on 12/17/33
18. The Bears and the Giants
19. 36th year
20. 63 yards

11 - Tragedy and Inconsistency: 1964-67
1. Dick Evey
2. Six
3. Halfback
4. 400
5. Through a trade with the Rams
6. Three
7. Phoenix Junior College
8. Two
9. University of Georgia
10. Quarterback
11. Four
12. Steve DeLong
13. DeLong signed with the AFL's San Diego Chargers
14. Michigan State
15. Seven

16. Fullback
17. Wisconsin
18. Six seasons
19. Wake Forest
20. Beattie Feathers
21. Four years
22. Lung cancer
23. Linebacker
24. Indiana
25. Three
26. 1967
27. Nine
28. 312

12 - A New Era: 1968-73
1. 20-36
2. Paddy Driscoll
3. Mike Hull
4. Fullback
5. USC
6. 12 times for 22 yards
7. Cecil Turner
8. Flanker
9. California State Polytechnic College
10. Green Bay Packers
11. The Bears
12. 13-10
13. Green Bay
14. 25
15. 25 extra points
16. Eight teams
17. U. of Kansas
18. 6.62 yards per carry
19. 6.87
20. Eight
21. 20
22. One
23. Five
24. 42%
25. 5.51 yards per pass
26. 30
27. 47.6
28. 51
29. Seven
30. Cincinnati Bengals
31. 1969
32. 15
33. 24.2
34. Twice
35. Lee Roy Caffey, Bob Hyland and Elijah Pitts
36. State Street Jack
37. Dallas Cowboys
38. One year

39. UCLA
40. End
41. Four
42. 33
43. Russ Montgomery
44. 229 yards
45. U. of Missouri
46. 1971
47. Two seasons
48. Philadelphia Eagles
49. Two years
50. Running back
51. TCU (Texas Christian University)
52. It was a bad snap from center and the holder, quarterback Bobby Douglas, threw the ball into the end zone, where it was caught by linebacker Dick Butkus.
53. 10 seasons
54. Cleveland for six years and Philadelphia for two years
55. Ron Smith
56. 31 yards
57. Eastern Kentucky University
58. First round
59. 1973
60. Defensive lineman
61. Five seasons
62. Cornerback
63. Second round
64. New England
65. Jack Brickhouse (Play by Play) & Irv Kupcinet (color)

13 - And Along Came Sweetness: 1974-79
1. U. of Tulsa
2. defensive back
3. Notre Dame
4. The Calgary Stampeders in the Canadian Football League
5. 1955
6. Nine
7. August 24, 1983
8. Jerry Vainisi
9. #7
10. Maryland University
11. 10 years
12. Guard
13. Tampa
14. #65
15. 992
16. Eight
17. Louisiana Tech

18. Safety
19. Notre Dame
20. 10 years
21. 629
22. 128
23. Third
24. Four
25. 62.4 %
26. 78.5%
27. Seven
28. Nine
29. Lake Forest College
30. Alan Page
31. 11.5
32. 10
33. Seven
34. Henderson Junior College
35. 50
36. Bo Rather
37. 39
38. 685
39. U. of Wisconsin
40. Tackle
41. Six
42. Yale
43. #45
44. Fred Caito
45. Tom Wilkinson
46. Six
47. Washington
48. Defensive coach
49. Eight years
50. Waymond Bryant
51. Tennessee State *
52. Mike Adamle
53. Two
54. #20
55. Two
56. Seven
57. LA Raiders
58. Doug Buffone
59. 14 seasons
60. 186 games
61. Gary Fencik
62. Five years
63. Bob Avellini

14 - The Iron Mike Era: 1982-92
1. Richard Dent
2. Tennessee State
3. Vestee Jackson
4. Nine years
5. Clemson
6. 13 years

7. Texas
8. Green Bay Packers
9. 12 years
10. Baylor
11. Four
12. Florida
13. Eight years
14. Louisville
15. Seven years
16. 18
17. 1985
18. 97.8
19. 1984
20. Twice
21. Mike Tomczak
22. Three
23. 12
24. 90
28. Second round
29. 1990
33. 21
34. Third
35. Dennis Gentry
36. 192
37. 22.7 yards per return
38. 200
39. 1981-88
40. 14
41. 4.4
42. None
43. 114
44. 307
45. Five
46. One year
47. Nate Lewis
48. 35
49. Steve Walsh
50. 14
51. Erik Kramer
52. Mark Bortz
53. 13
54. Curtis Conway and Johnny Bailey

15 - Rebuilding Again: 1993-Present
1. Four years
2. Four years
3. U. of Pittsburgh
4. Green Bay Packers
5. Tampa Bay
6. 47-17
7. Four
8. 144
9. 1985
10. 38

Chicago Bears Facts & Trivia

11. 25 yards
12. 29 yards
13. 82-61-6
14. 54-25-6

A Few Good Bears

1 - Mike Ditka
1. The first tight end inducted into the Hall of Fame
2. 56
3. Five times
4. Fifth round
5. Three times, winning once
6. Three times receiving and twice in scoring
7. #89

2 - Dick Butkus
1. Nine seasons
2. 25
3. Second
4. Five
5. 11
6. Third
7. 1966
8. Eight
9. U. of Illinois
10. 1979
11. Actor and football commentator

3 - Gale Sayers
1. Dick Butkus
2. Two seasons, 1966 & 1969
3. 20
4. 5.0 yards
5. Kansas
6. Fourth pick overall
7. 21, 7, 50, l yards
8. 80-yard screen pass
9. 85-yard punt return
10. Ernie Nevers of the Cardinals and Dub Jones of the Browns
11. 867
12. #40
13. 4,956 yards, fourth on the all time Bears list
14. Once
15. $50,000

4 - The Gallopin' Ghost
1. Wheaton, Illinois
2. #77

3. Seven seasons
4. The New York Yankees of the American Football League
5. The Bears
6. Defensive Back
7. 1931
8. C.C. Pyle
9. The Wheaton Ice Man
10. Cash and Carry
11. Candy bar, cigarettes, yeast foam malted milk, doll, fountain pen, ginger ale, sweaters, cap, shoes, socks
12. President Calvin Coolidge
13. 9-5-3

About the Author

Wayne Mausser was born near "The Field of Dreams" in Iowa and has spent the last 17 years of his adult life in radio, the last 11 as sports director for several stations. He has hosted numerous football programs involving professional players. He also hosts "Countdown to Kickoff", a one-hour pre-game football show with Ray Scott and currently works for radio station WPKR in Oshkosh, Wisconsin, and the Sports America Radio Network, located near "The Field of Dreams" in Dyersville, Iowa. His personal interests include collecting sports memorabilia.